Personality
and
Spiritual Freedom

Personality
and
Spiritual Freedom

ROBERT and CAROL ANN FAUCETT

Foreword by Abbot David Geraets, O.S.B.

Image Books
A Division of
Doubleday
New York
1987

We wish to dedicate this,
our first book,
to Father John Sheehan, S.M.,
who has gently, yet consistently,
invited us into the inner journey.

Acknowledgments
All scriptural quotes are taken from *The New Jerusalem Bible*,
copyright © 1985 by Darton, Longman & Todd, Ltd., and
Doubleday & Company, Inc. Used with permission of the
publisher.

Library of Congress Cataloging in Publication Data

Faucett, Robert, 1943–
Personality and spiritual freedom.

Bibliography: p. 147.
1. Spiritual life—1960–   . 2. Myers-Briggs Type
Indicator. 3. Christianity—Psychology. I. Faucett,
Carol Ann, 1945–   . II. Title.
BV4509.5.F38 1987   201'.9   87–5460
ISBN 0-385-24259-X

Contents

CONTENTS

Part II: The Value of Typology

Part III: Growth and Spirituality

Foreword

The concept of psychological types, as Carl Jung saw it, helps us deal with the complexities of relating to other people. The theory appears simple enough at first glance, but as with other attempts to clarify reality, when we study the material in depth the subject becomes more involved and the application broadens in scope.

What the Faucetts have accomplished is to present the theory in a way that facilitates understanding and at the same time elicits awareness of the spiritual implications that can be derived from this part of Jung's work. I trust that as you study these pages the Holy Spirit will be at work enlightening you to the truth of this, another facet of God's Kingdom.

DAVID GERAETS, O.S.B.
March 31, 1987

Introduction

Each of us is aware of so many facets of the world. We are aware of much of what goes on around us. The world, politics, our family or community. We are aware of the people with whom we work and play and live. But the aspect of the world with which we are most familiar, with which we are most intimate, is our own personality. We live with ourself every waking hour. Over time we have learned how we tick, how we behave in certain circumstances, the things about ourself we like and those we dislike. We know the type of activities we are drawn to and those from which we run.

This personality of ours, the way we behave, is unique to us. No one is just like us and no one knows us as well as we do. While we don't know *why* we behave as we do, we each hold a more intimate understanding of ourself than anyone else. We know many of our deepest desires. We know the pains we suffer, the joys we celebrate, the little idiosyncrasies that make us unique. We are uniquely ourself. No one is quite like us.

Yet, for as much as we know, there is far more that we don't know. There are deeply mysterious parts of ourself that also influence who we are and how we behave.

While we are intimately familiar with this personality of ours, its Creator often seems far away and mysterious. We try to move closer to him in many ways, such as learning about

him, praying to him, seeing him in others, and doing our best
to move forward on this Christian journey.

The good news we have here is the intimate connection
between this often distant and mysterious God and the intimately familiar reality of our own personality. Here, in our
unique and familiar day in and day out life, we find a deep
connection to the mysterious reality of God. The connection is
that this God we seek is the same God who created us. But he
created us uniquely in his own image! We were not fashioned
in some haphazard way by a roll of the genetic dice.

We are fashioned in the image and likeness of the Creator.
Thus, as we learn more about the creature—ourself—we learn
more about the Creator—God. Using as a tool the most familiar aspect of our world, our own personality, we learn more
about the most mysterious part of life—God.

As we probe and touch the various characteristics of our
own unique behavior, we cross over to the dimension of the
Divine. We can see and touch characteristics of our Lord. The
more we probe and touch these characteristics, the more we
begin to see that we know only a small portion of ourself. We
find there is much more than we expected to find in our personality and thus it becomes a rich gateway to a significant
spiritual journey—a journey that will take us to the Father
through the Son.

Jesus tells us he is the Good Shepherd. "I am the gate," he
tells us. "Anyone who enters through me will be safe: such a
one will go in and out and will find pasture" (John 10:9). Jesus
is the gate through which we must pass. Jesus, in his humanity,
also passed through the gate of who he was, his own personality, to find the Father and fulfill the Father's plan for him.

It would be reasonable to expect that the Christian who is
taking his or her faith seriously should be able to expect a life
with less conflict and more fruitful spiritual growth. However,
for many of us, that is not our experience. Over time, we begin
to see more and more of our own faults, the shortcomings of
others, and we begin to have a sense of our own brokenness.

Beginning to see our own failings is a sure sign of the presence of God's grace in our lives and of our spiritual growth.
Reaching a point of helplessness can open us to the grace of

the Spirit to show us what we need to know to make fruitful changes in our lives.

Many who will pick up this book are at that point. They see their failings and their brokenness but are unable to make the changes they believe they must. Still others have a desire to better understand themselves as a continuing part of their spiritual journey. All of this is evidence of God's abundant grace at work in their lives. But the ability to accept that grace requires an openness and, most importantly, a freedom—a freedom to make the difficult behavior changes that are often necessary.

We believe this freedom, which is a deep *spiritual freedom*, comes only after *acceptance*—acceptance of who we are and how we are made in the image of that mysterious God. This is the focus of this book. To understand and accept the gift of our personality—how we are made—and, in that acceptance, to grow in our freedom to behave according to the gifts of that same God-given personality and, when appropriate, in opposition to the natural preferences of that personality.

Personality

As a child, we look around and see that people are different from ourself. Certainly they *look* different. Most are big and we are small. Some have characteristics that identify them as either the same sex as ourself, or the "other" sex. So we learn that the world is filled with people who are like ourself yet unlike ourself. But we also learn that these differences or similarities in sex and appearance are not sufficient to form judgments about whether we like or dislike them.

Later, we learn that there are other differences. Aunt Sue is somewhat like our mother and we like that. Granddad hugs us and laughs and talks to us and we like that too. Uncle Henry speaks harshly and scolds us, and we don't like that! Now we learn that there are other differences and we can and do form judgments about who we are going to like and dislike. We are discovering differences known as personality.

Then, for many of us, a long time later, we begin to grow in awareness of ourself and become more conscious of how we behave. This awareness comes to each of us at different times and for different reasons. For some it comes as a result of a crisis in our life. Often from what seems to be a crisis of relationships in our marriage, family, work, or community. For others the awareness comes about through our Christian conversion, a time when we make a mature, adult commitment to Jesus Christ as Lord and Savior. Still, for others, it is impossible to pinpoint the reason for this heightened interest and awareness in our own personality. We now have, through desire and ability, a stronger interest in better understanding our own and the personality of others.

We may begin to compare ourself with those around us. We see characteristics in others that we both like and dislike and we make both conscious and unconscious comparisons with ourself. Perhaps we find these characteristics significantly more irritating or significantly more pleasant and appealing than in the past. We begin to ask ourself, "Why am I like that?" or "Why can't I be like him or her?" For some of us these are the same questions we asked when we were teenagers and we had too many pimples and were too short or too tall or too skinny or too fat and everyone was more popular and more beautiful or more handsome or more hip. But now we are really distressed, because we are thirty-five or sixty and we don't know why it bothers us so.

The flip side of the same coin has us unable to look at our own personality but focused on those around us. We ask, "Why does my husband (or wife) have to be that way?" Or we tell ourselves, "If only the pastor (or leader or superior) would act more reasonably, life would be so much better." We find ourself unable or unwilling to take any responsibility for the tensions in our life.

There is much to gain from understanding personality. Gaining self-knowledge and the resultant knowledge about God is only the beginning. We can also learn to accept ourself with all the frailties and brokenness we find. But even more, we can better live out the Gospel call to "love one another" (John 15:12). Loving one another can mean we accept that others are also made in the image and likeness of the Creator, though different from ourself. Then we can begin to live and love in harmony and acceptance. We can become more productive with those with whom we work. We can make better quality decisions by understanding the gifts and limitations of our personality and those around us. We can channel the energies of our ministries in areas that are better suited to our unique personality.

We offer this subject of Typology not as psychologists, but as qualified lay Christians who have endeavored to make use of the subject of personality in our own lives and ministry. We are married twenty-three years and have two college-age children. Bob was an executive with the Bell System for twenty years and together we now operate Look Beyond Ministries, our full-time vocation through which we offer parish missions, retreats, and workshops.

Over the past eleven years we have been extensively involved in various forms of lay ministry. After a twelve-year absence, our church involvement began following a Marriage Encounter Weekend and introduction to a fully alive parish in 1976. We have extensive training and experience in youth ministry, family ministry, marriage preparation, and parish leadership. We have held various positions in our diocese of Metuchen, New Jersey, as head of the Evangelization Commission and serving on the bishop's Pastoral Council.

Look Beyond Ministries was formed in 1978 from our home, which served as a center offering retreats for families and young people, days of recollection, Christian concerts, plus workshops and other events. During that time we coordinated and developed most of those programs along with others in our local community.

In 1984, with the blessing of our bishop, Theodore E. McCarrick—now Archbishop of Newark—Bob resigned from AT&T, and Look Beyond Ministries became our full-time vocation. Since then we have traveled extensively on a free-lance basis, offering retreats and parish missions on the topic of prayer and workshops for church leaders and religious communities, using the subject of this book—personality.

We were introduced to personality study as part of Bob's management training in the Bell System. The individual and spiritual value became quickly evident in our own lives as we began to incorporate the insights gained in our relationships with each other, our children, and those with whom we worked and played.

The specific theory we will use and explain in detail is known as Typology and utilizes the well-known *Myers-Briggs Type Indicator* (MBTI). The MBTI is a sophisticated personality questionnaire which helps begin the process of allowing one to pinpoint certain very positive and extremely helpful personality characteristics. As we grow in our understanding of these characteristics, we grow in our understanding that we are made in the image of God, yet each of us is different from our spouse, friend, or co-worker. It is here that we can grow in our self-awareness and in our love and acceptance of others who are different from ourself.

Both of us have extensive training in Typology and spirituality. Carol Ann is a graduate of the School for Spiritual Directors offered at the Benedictine Abbey in Pecos, New Mexico. She also has background in youth ministry from Seton Hall University. Bob is a graduate of the School for Spiritual Development offered by the Archdiocese of New York and both of us have extensive training in Ignatian spirituality and have experienced the forty-day Institute of the Spiritual Exercises at Loyola House in Guelph, Ontario. While not psychologists, we are professionally qualified Myers-Briggs consultants.

Understanding personality differences has proved to be very helpful to the thousands who have attended our workshops. Yet workshops are available to only a select few. Even those attending have expressed a need for something more. While a number of books have been written on the topic from both secular and Christian perspectives, we could not recommend a good Christian primer on the subject.

It is to meet this need that we set out to write this book. We have written with the intention that our work be simple and understandable. In addition, we have tried to take into consideration the deep spiritual richness we, and many others, have found in Dr. Carl Jung's theory of Typology. We do so with the encouragement of Bob Heller of Doubleday, and Fr. Chris Aridas of the Diocese of Rockville Center, New York, both of whom have been instrumental in making this book a reality.

We also thank the community at the Benedictine Abbey of Our Lady of Guadalupe, Pecos, New Mexico, and Frs. Thomas E. Clarke, S.J., and Joseph Lynch, S.M., who made some very helpful suggestions.

Our book is designed first and foremost as a primer. Whether you have no information or a wealth of information on the subject, it is meant to take you through a basic and simple explanation of Typology as it pertains to an active Christian. The book is in three parts. At the conclusion of Part I you should have a basic understanding of the theory and thus be on your way to applying it to your own personality. Part II will offer applications: how to put the theory to use in our own life, our relationships with others, and our relationship with God. Part III will explore the richly rewarding and spiritual aspects of growth and maturity and will include ideas that can be helpful to the reader's prayer style. We will see how we grow and change as we move through the various stages of life, including mid-life, and will begin to see why our personality is not the same when we are twelve as twenty-five or sixty. We will see the promise of integration and wholeness that can be found in applying the lessons of personality to ourself.

Typology has been for us both a gift and a tool to a deeper relationship with God, a greater self-understanding, and a help in living out the Christian call to love one another. It has offered a new dimension in our journey to God and a passage-way into an ever-unfolding spiritual awakening. God has opened doors to the inner journey, the symbolic, and to a greater acceptance of our weaknesses and our strengths. We truly pray that you, our readers, will allow Jesus to mold you and melt you, to enlighten you and to draw you into a deeper understanding of the spiritual freedom he intends for each of us.

How to Use This Book

This book is intended to be used by an individual reader or as a resource for group study. These groups might well be a work group, that is, a group that works together in some task, perhaps a council, committee, or team of some sort. On the other hand, the group could be a community, that is, a group that lives together. It could be a family, religious community, or other group that is convenanted in some way.

At the end of most of the short chapters there are reflection questions. If a group is studying the subject together, the individuals should reflect on the questions alone, then come together to share their findings or discoveries. As a final group sharing, members might simply reflect upon the question "What impact does this information have on our group?" If we are honest, it is likely that much of the later chapters will have significant impact, especially chapter 9, "The Value of Typology for Community."

PART I

Understanding Typology

1

Typology—Some Background

In the Gospel writing of St. John, Jesus calls us to love one another. This is a central message of our Christian faith. Typology, the subject of this book, can help us come to a better understanding and appreciation of one another and in that way help us to better put into practice the message of Jesus in our everyday dealings with other people. Let us look at some everyday situations.

Case 1

A married couple begins to notice differences in how they act with their friends. The wife wants to be with their friends much more frequently than the husband, and she comes home after a party full of energy. He, on the other hand, would prefer less social contacts. After he goes to a party he comes home and is ready to collapse. He *and* she begin to wonder if something is wrong with him.

Case 2

The staff of St. Andrew's parish meets over lunch each week to discuss liturgy, programs, and parish education efforts. Director of Religious Education Mary Ellen is full of new ideas she just brought from a conference and presents them in an enthusiastic, energetic way. The staff seems to share her enthusiasm and even Pastor Edward appears to nod agreement after he asks some very detailed implemental questions. Mary Ellen and the staff leave the meeting feeling confident she has a mandate to implement the idea. Father Ed, on the other hand, is patiently expectant that more information will be forthcoming at next week's meeting so other ideas, as well as Mary Ellen's, can be discussed. Next week's gathering will be a shock to both Mary Ellen and Father Ed when they discover the different impressions they took from the previous meeting.

Case 3

A convent is occupied by ten sisters, some of whom work in the parish school and some in various apostolates outside the convent. When they come together for the periodic community meetings, Sr. Jean wants very much to share struggles and joys in her apostolate and to hear the same from the other sisters. Sr. Margaret wants to stay with the business of running the convent. Sr. Jean sees Sr. Margaret as cold and impersonal, while Sr. Margaret can't understand why Sr. Jean doesn't see the necessity of staying with the agenda and getting the work done. She thinks Sr. Jean should save all that "personal material" for her spiritual director.

Case 4

A group of religious education teachers are gathered for a meeting to plan the activities of the coming year. John is leading the discussion and is very much interested in the specific plans for efficiently arranging the liturgies and the penance services and special activities for Advent and Lent. He wants very much to stay with the same program as last year because it worked so well and all the details are already in order in last year's file. Several others agree. There are a few at the meeting who really think that it is time for some changes to be made. They want to try some new ideas. They offer many interesting possibilities, but John and his allies begin to list all the reasons why these new ideas are bound to fail, and the meeting grinds to a halt. Each group holds firmly to its position.

All of these situations are helpfully explained when we begin to understand personality differences. As we study this complex and interesting subject, we can see that the differences we find in situations such as those above are not caused by one person being right and the other wrong, but simply a variety of equally good ways of living our lives.

We can begin to understand and accept differences in energy level, like our married couple in Case 1, with their different needs for sociability. They have found for themselves—as others have discovered—that interaction with a lot of people is draining for the husband and energizing for the wife.

With Fr. Ed and Mary Ellen, in the second case, we see their different approaches to interacting with the world. Fr. Ed takes plenty of time with decisions and wants to be sure he has all the information before he decides. On the other hand, Mary Ellen wants to get the "show on the road" and thus makes her decisions as soon as possible.

Sr. Jean's and Sr. Margaret's tensions arise from another pair of personality differences. Sr. Jean desires to share her life with others near to her and is more aware of her fellow sisters and their feelings. Sr. Margaret is not as at home in that sort of sharing and may be uncomfortable dealing with her own and others' feelings. She excels at being logical and firm-minded in her decisions.

In our final group of religion teachers, we see how the two groups have different ways of taking in and analyzing information. John and those who prefer leaving things status quo depend more on their experience of the past. The other group dislikes repetition and wants to use their imagination to come up with new ways of doing things.

As we better understand these personality differences, we can see that God has made a rich assortment of personalities. We are able to understand that some of our own traits are not "abnormalities," but part of our uniqueness and giftedness. So too, when we see others' unique gifts we are better able to accept them "where they are" and grow from our differences. We can even laugh when we appreciate the humorous variety that God has placed in our lives.

The value of understanding personalities lies in accepting myself as being unique and made in *God's image and likeness.* Part of that acceptance is to see those who are different from me as equally good and unique. The paradox is that once we accept the gift of how we have been made, only then can we begin to change and become all that God has intended for us.

Each of us contains the capacity for a wide range of behaviors, talents, attitudes, and feelings that are far above the ones we use on a daily basis. We each hold an untapped reservoir of abilities that we don't recognize as being part of ourselves. St. Paul seems to speak of this in his prayer to the Ephesians when he says, "In the abundance of his glory may he, through his Spirit, enable you to grow firm in power with regard to your hidden self . . ." (Ephesians 3:16). This "hidden self" of which St. Paul speaks is the reservoir upon which we will draw as we study our personalities. We will probe and learn of abilities and gifts that lie hidden deep within us. As we grow in knowledge of this hidden self, we grow in our freedom to use tools and capacities we didn't even know we had.

But using these newly found tools takes freedom. The freedom to choose our behavior from our expanded full range of possibilities. The goal of this book is just that—*freedom.*

For thousands of years, humans have sought to explain and classify the obvious differences in human personalities. One need only look at those around us to substantiate the claim that *people are different from one another.* The philosopher Hippocrates sought to explain these differences with his theory of four temperaments. He spoke of persons being melancholic, phlegmatic, choleric, or sanguine. A tribute to the basic truth in his theory is found in its existence after two thousand years.

Modern psychology is only about a hundred years old, but it takes its roots from centuries of man's quest to understand human behavior. Going back to the ancient philosophers and mythologies of many cultures, we find various attempts by man to touch and explain the mysterious depths of personality and human behavior.

Carl Gustav Jung, who lived from 1875 to 1961, was a noted Swiss psychiatrist who began his career as a protégé of Sigmund Freud. He ultimately broke with Freud over the issue of the importance of sex in determining human behavior.

Jung has the distinction of being one of the few noted secular psychological theorists who is "friendly" to religion. At the end of his life, when asked about his own belief in God, he replied, "I *know*. I don't need to believe. I know." For many psychologists, religion is a creation of humans to meet their own needs. Faith is explained away and is tolerated in analysis only as it meets this need. This is not to say that we, as Christians, cannot learn from such psychologists. We simply have to understand their perspective when we listen to their ideas.

Jung was not an orthodox Christian, but his positive attitude toward the religious experience allows us to be receptive to what he said along spiritual/psychological lines. We will not be discussing his theology here but, rather, bringing the gift of his theory of Typology into the Christian experience.

We are on a journey—a journey to God. As we grow and change throughout our lives, we have the opportunity to grow in the fullness of our personality, to become all that God intends for us as his children.

God has made each of us unique and in his own image. Indeed, the personality characteristics, as described within this book, are not some "right" and some "wrong" but, rather, *all right*—all in God's image. Many of us have gone through life seeing parts of our own characteristics as being "out of kilter" with the rest of society, seeing ourselves as somehow wrong and inferior to those around us. In fact, as we will see, each culture tends to support and reject certain personalities as being either good or bad, acceptable or unacceptable. In this way, our culture "sends us messages" about our personality characteristics as being "right" or "wrong."

In the book of Genesis, we read: "God created man in the image of himself, in the image of God he created him, male and female he created them" (1:27). We see Typology as a tool to draw us to wholeness, a tool to help us strive for our full potential as children of God.

We are not suggesting that all behavior is socially or morally cceptable. What we hope to show is that our natural behavior "preferences," that is, ways we like to behave in given circumstances, are natural and part of God's image in which we are created. As with all of God's gifts, our use of them has the potential to be either sinful or virtuous.

The freedom we are offered here is a freedom to accept these natural preferences as gifts, as potential sources for growth, and as tools to enable us to live out more fully the *Gospel values* that Jesus has shown us—Gospel values such as loving one another, forgiving our enemies, and spreading the Good News. In fact, Jesus's life will be used throughout to illustrate the acceptability and "God likeness" of the various aspects of human behavior. If Jesus shows us the Father (John 8:19), then we can use his life as our example of how to live. Jesus had the freedom to choose the action that was appropriate to his situation. We see that at times he needed to be strong and assertive, as when he expelled the money changers from the temple (Matthew 21:12–17). We also see those times when he acted in quite the opposite way of being understanding and compassionate, when the woman caught in adultery was brought before him (John 8:3–11). He didn't condemn her but loved her and asked her to correct her life.

The Christian Journey—Toward Wholeness

God created us body, mind, and spirit, and he desires wholeness for each of us. In the Gospels we have evidence of Jesus's desire for bodies to be whole in his meeting the physical needs of such as Jairus's daughter (Luke 8:49–56) and the woman with the hemorrhage (Matthew 9:20–22). We also see how God desires to bring us to wholeness of mind and emotions when Jesus forgives the adulterous woman (John 8:3–11). In Matthew's eighth chapter, we see Jesus casting out the devils (Matthew 8:28–34) and here we see evidence of his desire for spiritual healing. Among the many other "healing" accounts, we can see how clearly Jesus calls us to this "wholeness" of all of our faculties. This is indeed the Good News.

In our own day, we continue to see this evidence of physical, emotional, and spiritual healing by God. God still heals his people physically. There are many who have been healed of sicknesses. In addition, many of us have had experiences of hurt and pain both when we were growing up and in our adult lives. There have been times when people have hurt us by their words or actions. Through time, prayer, and ministry we may have had those painful memories healed and may even become thankful for that past.

Finally, there are millions today who attest to a deep spiritual healing through moments of conversion or metanoia, of being "born again." These are powerful healing experiences resulting in grace-filled changes of mind and heart. Many, who were away from God and Church, return to a deep personal relationship with Jesus and a more abundant life. It is precisely this *abundant life* that Jesus calls us to in the Gospel and in this inner journey: "I have come so that they may have life and have it to the full" (John 10:10). The Amplified version reads: "I came that they may have and enjoy life, and have it in abundance—to the full—till it overflows."[1]

We all have much growing to do, and God has placed that deep desire to grow within each of us. As we grow in acceptance of ourself, grow in holiness and fullness of life, keeping our eyes upon Jesus, our love of ourself and the way we love our neighbor will grow in balance and harmony.

Conscious and Unconscious

Each of us is made up of a conscious and an unconscious. The conscious is that part of ourself of which we are aware. In computer language, it is sort of like our "current memory." Right now you are *aware* of a certain part of your own identity —perhaps that you are married or single, a man or a woman. You are aware of your body, any pains or discomfort, you are aware of your environment, the temperature, the season, whether you are indoors or out, etc. This is some of the material of your conscious. Most theories maintain this "conscious" is only about 10 percent of our total being, and both Freud and Jung referred to the center of this conscious mind as the ego.

But, the other 90 percent is a much greater part of your

being which resides in your unconscious. That is the part of your self of which you are *not currently aware.* It is an enormous field of energy and power which is out of sight. It is

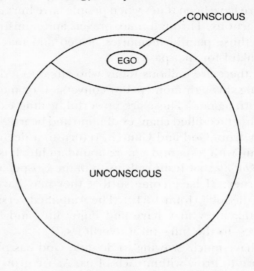

THE TOTAL BEING

filled with all of your memories, experiences, personality, and more. They are, for the moment, hidden and unavailable to your conscious mind. The fact that they are hidden by no means denotes that they have no effect on your behavior. It is here in the unconscious that all of those behaviors, talents, attitudes, and feelings we spoke of above reside. But in addition, our unconscious has a gremlin-like effect upon us and most of us can identify with St. Paul when he said, "I do not act as I mean to, but I do things that I hate" (Romans 7:15). It is the contents of this hidden unconscious that have so much effect on our behavior. They are so hidden that the conscious mind, the ego, denies their very existence. As we move forward, we will find in our unconscious a deep source of renewal, growth, strength, and wisdom.

The Myers-Briggs Type Indicator

Carl Jung began work on his theory of Typology as early as 1913, and his ideas were translated into English in 1923. His theory was developed to clarify the personality differences he had studied and noted in many of his clients. He was drawn to this work as an answer to the question "Why are people different?" From 1923 to 1941, Katherine Briggs and her daughter Isabel Briggs Myers studied Jungian theory and personality in detail. From 1941 to 1956, they spent enormous resources in an effort to develop an instrument to identify personality characteristics they had noted in Jung's work. Following testing, interviews, revision, and study, the Myers-Briggs Type Indicator (MBTI) was published as a research tool in 1962 by Educational Testing Services of Princeton, New Jersey.

In 1975, Consulting Psychologists Press, of Palo Alto, California, took over the publishing of the indicator and, since then, its use has grown dramatically. The MBTI is a psychological instrument as widely used as any other in the world. The publisher states that over 1.5 million copies were sold in 1986, and that represented a 23 percent increase over 1985. Unique to this instrument is a large national organization known as APT, the Association for Psychological Type in Gainesville, Florida.[2] The association is a network organization for persons interested in Typology and is growing at a rate of 25 percent annually. It now has nearly three thousand members.

The MBTI is used by both secular and religious organizations for a variety of applications. Some use it for counseling in career, individual, family, and marital situations. Others use it for team or community building applications.

Taking the Myers-Briggs

Many readers who have gone through a workshop have undoubtedly taken the MBTI and, hopefully, have their results in hand. The ethics of the publisher and practitioner insist that those taking the Indicator have the opportunity to meet with a qualified consultant to walk through the results in the event there is disagreement or need for clarification. For this reason, the Myers-Briggs is not available through the mail, and certain qualifications must be met to purchase and administer the instrument. Though a simplified self-scored indicator can be found in the David Keirsey–Marilyn Bates book, *Please Understand Me,*[3] it is best to locate a qualified consultant to administer the MBTI and be available for the feedback.

The Eight Functions and Attitudes

In the four chapters which follow we will discuss in detail four pairs of characteristics measured by the MBTI. They are as follows:

Introversion and Extraversion
Sensing and Intuiting
Thinking and Feeling
Judging and Perceiving

Each of these pairs are opposites. In other words, we cannot behave as both an introvert and an extravert at exactly the same time. We each have the capacity to be both, but at any given time we are using either one or the other. Also, each of us has a natural preference in using one over the other. This concept is best illustrated by the following exercise:

Take a piece of paper and write your full name using the hand with which you normally write. Now, transfer your pen or pencil to your opposite hand and write your full name again.

If you are like most people, words like awkward, slow, sloppy, and clumsy will best describe the second experience.

This is a good analogy for the pairs of preferences we will discuss in the following chapters. Each of us can use all of the characteristics, but we prefer to use one over the other, just as we prefer to use our right or left hand. If we choose or are forced to use the opposite characteristic, we will tend to find it "awkward, slow, sloppy, clumsy," etc. Simply put, one of each pair will be more available to us, as it is a part of our conscious being, and the other or opposite will reside more or less out of reach in our unconscious.

Each of us is given a unique set of gifts and limitations with which to work our way through life. Our goal is to develop to our fullest the gifts and strengths with which we are endowed. Ultimately, we are also called upon to develop the opposite or hidden characteristics, so that we are *free to choose appropriate behavior*. We will discuss this development and call to freedom in detail in chapters 10 and 11.

Finally, this tool of the Myers-Briggs is not a rigid absolute. It is to be used in conjunction with prayer, as we apply the concept to our life. As we grow in our understanding and awareness of who we are, with our many strengths and weaknesses, we will be moving forward on our journey to God. This journey will take a lifetime to fulfill.

NOTES

1. The Amplified Bible, published by Zondervan Publishing House, Grand Rapids, Mich., 1965.

2. The Association for Psychological Type, 2720 Northwest Sixth Street, Gainesville, FL 32609.

3. David Keirsey and Marilyn Bates, *Please Understand Me*, Prometheus Nemesis Books, P.O. Box 2082, Del Mar, CA 92014.

2

The Attitudes of Introvert and Extravert

The first pair of characteristics identified by Jung are the attitudes of introversion and extraversion. These are two words with which most of us are familiar, and our understanding can help in comprehending what Jung meant in his use of the terms. The basic characteristics he was describing have to do with how one is *energized*—from where one receives his or her energy. The extravert receives it from the *outer world,* while the introvert receives it from the *inner world.* This will become clear as we describe the pair.

Extraverts

The extraverts, or "E" in Myers-Briggs shorthand, comprise nearly 60 to 65 percent of the U.S. population and these are the folks who are generally the outwardly confident people. They like to be involved with the outer world of people, events and happenings. They are the *action people.* New experiences are an attractive challenge to the extravert. It is in trying new things that extraverts are able to understand them.

The extravert is sociable and comfortable with people. Extraverts can be so energized when they are involved with people that they can come home from a party or meeting full of energy. They may need time to "wind down" before going to bed.

The extravert often has to *speak* to get a handle on what they think or believe. Often thoughts are formed and convictions understood as they are being spoken. They can sometimes begin to talk about a rather profound subject and, when finished, register surprise at what they've said. People will laugh at this, but the words they spoke were often news to them too! When I (Bob), who am extraverted, begin pontificating on some subject, I often have to remind Carol Ann that I am just doing "some noisy thinking." "If I get to something important, I'll let you know."

On the other hand, it takes energy for the extravert to maintain solitude. To stay in a house with no one else home, they will probably turn on the TV or radio. Likewise, they might prefer the radio talk shows while driving alone.

Though the extravert's relationships are not usually at the same depth as are the introvert's, the extravert is likely to have a larger number of friends and acquaintances. As they like to be involved with people, they will get around and tend to "know everybody." This goes for their interests as well. The extravert is more likely to be interested in a host of different subjects, but he or she might not be into them as deeply as an introvert. They could well be the "jack of all trades and master of none."

Introverts

The introvert is one who needs to receive energy from the quiet or *inner world*. They comprise the other 35 to 40 percent of the U.S. population and they have a natural need to go "inside" to find their reserve. They take the world from outside and process it "inside." Thus they need more space, more solitude. For this reason, they often seem quieter than the extravert. But this is not always the case. Often, one who is introverted also has an "outgoing" personality. They might give the appearance of being extraverted, but when it comes to *energy*, they must tap that well *inside*.

This is the case for me (Carol Ann). As an introvert, I can appear to be very extraverted leading a weekend workshop, but I need much more time and space than Bob does before and after to receive my required energy. Bob, on the other hand, is frequently "fired up" after a conference. An extravert is not always the super-outgoing noisy type. They can be quiet, just as an introvert can be outgoing. The determining factor is *how each receives their energy.*

The introvert is more interested in the inner world, that is, the inner world of themselves and others, of ideas, concepts, thoughts, and feelings. They are likely to pursue more solitary activities and often like working alone, or with only a few people. They often find themselves fired up with energy following times of being quietly alone. They usually desire and allow for more quiet time, and can sometimes seem to be aloof.

The introvert needs time and space to make decisions and process information and they will frequently dislike interruptions. Unlike the extravert who "thinks out loud," the introvert needs to go inside to figure out what he or she thinks and believes. As with all of these characteristics, this has nothing to do with intelligence. It is simply a matter of preferred behavior.

As a married team comprised of an extravert and an introvert, I (Bob) have learned to give Carol Ann "space" when a decision needs to be made. I tend to make decisions faster, while Carol Ann needs more time.

Recently we were in an audio store to buy a tape recorder for our work. The young "high tech" salesman found us the appropriate model but then began to press for a decision. While I could have bought it right away, Carol Ann needed a bit of time and space to make up her mind. After walking around the store for a bit, she was better able to make her decision.

The introvert prefers the intimacy of one-to-one relationships. They are likely to have fewer friends than the extravert, but those friendships tend to be deeper and more intimate and perhaps much more important to them. The introvert is more apt to feel lonely in a crowd of strangers. If they go to a large party, it is likely to be a "draining" experience for them. As we've said, their preference is for activities that involve few or no people. They can be at ease by themselves and are "comfortable in their own company."

They may find spontaneous large-group sharing difficult, as verbal communication skills are often not one of their strengths, but, again, this is not universal. Introverts will need to be *invited* to share what they are thinking where an extravert is more likely to jump right in.

It is for these same reasons that introverts often have more difficulty with conflict and confrontation. The very thought of provoking an argument with someone could be enough to send them to their place of quiet. The extravert, on the other hand, may be one who brags that they love a good argument. They are often at their best when they have to think "on their feet."

Jesus—Introvert or Extravert?

How about Jesus? Was he introverted or extraverted? Scripture shows Jesus clearly using both characteristics. On one hand, he was comfortable with many people. He preached to thousands, and he had a community of twelve disciples, which would be a large number for an introvert. He was able to go and dine with strangers and sinners. This, too, takes extraverted energy.

On the other hand, we see Jesus going off to the mountains to pray. Like an introvert, he needed time to "recharge his batteries." His forty days in the desert were certainly not extraverted days! He also shows us his introversion by having a special, intimate friendship with just a few. We see him going off sometimes with Peter, James, and John, and this deeper relationship with a smaller number would be characteristic of an introvert.

Before we address more about Jesus's type, let us emphasize a very important point. *None of us is a pure introvert or extravert.* All of us are *blends.* The preferences are opposite. We cannot be introvert and extravert at the same time. To behave as an introvert, we must turn off our interaction with the outside world. In order to be an extravert, that is, *involved* with the outside world, we turn our attention away from what is going on inside.

Perhaps we can identify with the experience of our attention rapidly moving between both worlds, as we momentarily focus on what someone is saying to us and then "tune them out" as our attention moves to some thought or idea that catches our attention. Because our minds are so fast, we have the capacity to get enough of what the person is saying to understand them. But we cannot focus on both our inner thought and this "outside" person's words at the same instant. These two worlds are opposite.

However, we each use both characteristics. The most extraverted person in the world can and does go "inside" from time to time, just as the most introverted person has to "extravert." It is a matter of survival. We could not live in this world without both. Typology is a matter of *preference*. How do we *prefer* to behave? Which comes most natural? Do we naturally use our right hand or our left hand? Our introversion or our extraversion? We can and do use both. It is simply more natural to use one more than the other.

It is now appropriate to get a flavor of where we are going. We are moving toward *freedom*, freedom to choose our behavior. If I am naturally extraverted, without thinking about it, I am more often going to choose extraverted behavior. For example, let us say I am standing before two doors and deciding which one to open. I know that behind one there is a party and behind the other is a room with a chair and a good book. On the natural level, the extravert will prefer to choose the party door and the introvert will want to choose the quiet door.

However, there are times when we will need to choose the *opposite*. For his or her own growth and health, the extravert will need to choose a good book, and the introvert will need to choose a party. Fully participating in life includes both possibilities. To be whole, we need to have *the freedom to choose either*. If the gift God has given me is to be extraverted, I am called to accept my gift of extraversion and be a good extravert. But I am also called to wholeness. Thus, I am called to be introverted when circumstances deem it appropriate. This is the essence of the journey on which we have embarked, the journey to freedom, the journey to freely choose our behavior. Achieving this freedom is not a matter of simply making decisions. Freedom comes from practice, experience, and, ultimately, being attracted to that which was not formerly attractive to us. This is the promise of understanding our preferences, accepting them, developing them, and then, *in freedom,* acting against them when circumstances call us to do so.

Now let's get back to Jesus. Was he extraverted or introverted? Some would say he was the perfect balance, with a preference for neither one nor the other. We, along with many others, prefer the theory that in his humanity Jesus indeed did have a preference. If he was fully human, then he was fully endowed with a right hand and a left hand, and a preference for one over the other. Thus, he is likely to have had a preference for either extraversion or introversion. However, as the one ultimately most free, he had the most freedom to choose the attitude that was required by the circumstances in which he found himself. This is the freedom to which he calls each of us. We will speak more of Jesus's freedom and of our own in chapters 10 and 11.

Let us suggest, if you are not usually accustomed to using reflection questions that follow chapters in books, that it would be very helpful in this chapter and the three that follow (chapters 2–5) to use the questions to help you have an idea of your own type preference.

QUESTIONS FOR REFLECTION

1. Based on the description of the introvert and the extravert, what is your preference and how strong is that preference in your personality?

2. What are the main characteristics of this attitude that lead you to make this choice?

3. What do you think is the attitude, extravert or introvert, of the person who is closest to you? (spouse, friend, close relative, etc.)

4. What is a situation in which the preferences of both you and this person were evident?

5. If you had a free day, how would you spend it in an attempt to renew your energy?

3

The Functions of Sensing and Intuiting

This first pair of the two sets of functions deals with how one *perceives* or *takes in life*. Each of us prefers to let life come to us either through our "sensing" function or our "intuiting" function. The way we take in the world is of extreme importance to understanding our personality as we spend our entire waking life either receiving information or acting upon it. We could not make any decisions about life, business, relationships, God, or anything else if we did not first receive information upon which to act. The way we prefer to receive that information is the focus of this pair of functions.

The sensing function is identified by the Myers-Briggs shorthand of "S", and the intuiting function with an "N". (The "I" was already used for "Introvert.")

One who prefers to take in life with their sensing function chooses to take in *details*, while one who prefers the intuiting function prefers the world to come through *whole concepts or ideas*. Both of these functions are good. Both are made in the image of God. At the same time, none of us is pure sensing or intuiting. We are all blends of both. Just as we prefer to use one hand over the other, we prefer one function over the other. However, they are *opposites*. We cannot use both at the same time.

Consider a painting. If you wish to focus upon the details—the colors, texture, brushstrokes, etc.—it is necessary to look very closely. When we do so, we are unable to see the entire work. On the other hand, when we step back and view the whole picture, we have lost our focus on those details. These two processes alternately use the sensing and the intuiting functions. We can use only one of them at a time.

The Sensing Function

Approximately 75 percent of the U.S. population prefer to take in the world using their sensing function (represented by "S"). For the "senser," life and the world and their environment comes to them through their senses and from their personal experience of life. The five senses of seeing, hearing, smelling, touching, and feeling are their most preferred and dependable sources of perceiving.

For the senser, experience comes in the *details*, and their own personal experience is the most important part of their understanding of the world. As the senser is very attuned to the sensate details of their environment, they have the gift of living in the "here and now." For the senser, their preferred way to take in the world is to be *present* to what is going on around them. For this reason, the senser is unlikely to sacrifice the joy of the present moment for a promise of some future enjoyment.

The senser tends to love life and to enjoy it more than his or her intuitive counterpart. The sensers will be the "consumers" and pleasure-lovers. They will be attentive to others' enjoyment of life and tend to imitate them to take in that experience for themselves.

For example, some years ago we had the opportunity to fly out West for a once-in-a-lifetime family vacation of two weeks touring the National Parks and wonderment of the western United States. In order to do this we had to sacrifice some to the Christmas presents for our children. So on Christmas morning, we designed a wonderful surprise for the kids with brochures and posters to share what would take place next summer. While our intuitive son managed a half-hearted smile as he began to anticipate, our sensing daughter could not contain her disappointment. "You mean that's it? That's our big Christmas present? I'm going back to bed!" Now her two future-minded intuitive parents could not understand her disappointment. However, when the trip came, she was better equipped to really enjoy it and take in much more of the details of God's creation. She also remembers far more of the details of the trip than the rest of us.

The senser will likely be drawn to activities that are more detail-based. They will often be the bookkeeper or recording secretary in a group. They are the one who is more concerned with their possessions. They will have the neatest house, the polished car, the organized spice rack, and their tools on a nice neat Peg-Board.

Jesus's Use of Sensing

Jesus had the gift of presence. He was able to really be there for people and to perceive their needs. He listened to people and touched them. His message was "the kingdom of Heaven is close at hand" (Matthew 4:17)—*now*—in the present. This is a sensing message.

Our favorite sensing scripture (italics ours) is the first four verses of John's First Letter:

> Something which has existed since the beginning,
> which we have *heard,*
> which we have *seen with our own eyes,*
> which we have *watched*
> and *touched* with our own *hands.*
> The Word of life—
> this is our theme.
> That life was made *visible;*
> we *saw it* and are giving our testimony,
> declaring to you the eternal life,
> which was *present* to the Father
> and has been *revealed to us.*
> We are declaring to you
> what we have *seen and heard,*
> so that you too may share our life.
> Our life is shared with the Father

and with his Son Jesus Christ.
We are writing this to you so that *our joy may
be complete.*

In church history we can see the life of St. Francis and his
presence to nature and the animals. When he heard the Lord
call him to "rebuild my church," his response was to go out
and actually begin the reconstruction of a fallen-down building. This was a classic sensing response.

The Intuiting Function

Those who prefer to take in their environment with their intuiting function represent only about 25 percent of the U.S.
population. (Intuiting is written as "N" in Myers-Briggs language.)

For these individuals, life and ideas come in "whole pictures." That is, unlike the sensing types who get the "picture"
in a somewhat serial mode, through the details, the intuitives
get the "picture" or idea all at once without the associated
details.

The intuitives live life in an expectant mode, wondering,
craving inspiration, looking around the corner at what is yet to
come. They are the inventors. They are both imaginative and
creative. They are not constrained by the limitations of what is,
but tend to be dreamers and comfortable in thinking "what
if?" For this reason, they often excel when it comes to prob-
lem-solving.

The intuitives have a somewhat future orientation to their
lives. They have a more difficult time living in the "here and
now." For the intuitives, life is more "around the corner."
They think not so much in terms of what *is,* but what *could be* or
what *might be.* They often focus on the possibilities as opposed
to the present moment.

A classic illustration of this characteristic is found in both of
our own strong preferences for intuiting. Several years ago, as
part of our move to full-time ministry, we sold our former
house and, to save expense, built a new, much smaller one. We
took about five months off from our work and dedicated our-

selves to finishing it. One day, about two weeks before we moved in, we were painting and wallpapering. We took a break to eat. Suddenly, after talking a half hour, we burst out laughing. We had caught ourselves not living in the present, but talking about the *next house* we would build someday! After our having invested all that time, one would have thought we could at least have savored the moment of completion. But that is not the gift of the intuitive.

The intuitive can be happy in the world of symbols, for, again, unlike the sensing type, the symbols represent more to them than the literal symbol. The intuitive might take a walk in the woods and see the branches of a beautiful tree as reaching up to heaven, and its roots as symbolic of earthiness. They may be drawn to myths, dreams, and visions.

The intuitive will dislike details and may be annoyed by the senser's preoccupation with fine points and details. For the intuitive, the conclusion or "bottom line" is far more important than the route one used to get to that point, while the senser often cannot get to that same point until they have paced through each of the steps.

Jesus's Use of Intuiting

The most intuitive picture of Jesus is found in the symbolism of John's Gospel, where Jesus speaks of himself as the "bread of life" (6:35) and the "good shepherd" (10:11) and the "vine" (15:5). In church history, we need only look at a figure as recent as Pope John XXIII, whose visionary work called forth the Second Vatican Council. We can look at Martin Luther King, who had a vision of integration that came from his intuitive vantage point of the world. Both of these men saw life not as it was, but as it could be.

Contrast of the Two Functions

Those who prefer sensing are oriented to the present and their past experience rather than the intuitives' future outlook.

Those who prefer sensing base their beliefs more on their

own experience than the intuitives' ideas, which come from the speculative or their hunches.

Sensers prefer the present practical reality rather than what could be.

Sensing types will be reading this information wondering about the details, and how it applies to their present-day lives, while the intuitives are beginning to see the possibilities of the theory already. (Most of the people who are really involved in Typology are intuitives.)

While the sensers will care about the fine points and details, the intuitives will often feel their information is "close enough."

Sensers will ask questions such as "what if?" while intuitives will avoid such questions and be convinced that "it'll all work out."

QUESTIONS FOR REFLECTION

1. Based on the descriptions of sensing and intuiting, what is your preference and how strong is that preference in your personality?

2. What are the main characteristics of this function that lead you to make this choice?

3. What do you think is the function, sensing or intuiting, of the person closest to you? (spouse, friend, close relative, etc.)

4. What is a situation in which both you and this person's preferences were evident?

5. Do you spend more time concerned with what is going on around you *now*, or concerned with things *yet to come?* Explain.

4

The Functions of Thinking and Feeling

When we described sensing and intuiting, we noted that they were the functions with which we "perceive," or take in, the world. The next pair of functions, thinking and feeling, have to do with how we act upon the world. By this we imply the process we use to come to conclusions; a way of sorting out information or organizing the data we have gathered using our intuiting and sensing functions. As we act upon the world, we do so using either our thinking function or our feeling function.

Here again, while each of us can and does use both functions, they are opposites and we cannot use them both at the same time.

In the U.S. population, we find that 50 percent of the people prefer the thinking function, and 50 percent prefer the feeling function. However, there are other complications. Among the men, about 60 percent will prefer to use their thinking over feeling, and among the women about 65 percent will prefer the feeling function over thinking. As we explain these functions many will conclude that these percentages are "natural," as thinking is a man's style, and feeling seems to be more a woman's style. We wish to dispel that idea at the outset. While it is true that more men prefer thinking, and more women feeling, most will agree that a 60/40 split is not sufficient to warrant that sort of distinction.

The Thinking Function

Those who prefer to use the thinking function (represented by "T") in making decisions tend to prefer using logic, facts, and truth as opposed to values and relationships. We'll speak more of these decisions shortly, but let us make it clear that we are not speaking of "intelligence" here. We are talking of one who uses *their understanding* of facts, truth, and logic in making decisions. The function describes a preferred style of making decisions as opposed to the ability to "intelligently" apply all the facts. The thinker is apt to be able to organize facts and ideas somewhat logically. They seem to possess an ability to sequentially understand a situation.

If there is one word that best describes the focus of the thinker, it is *justice.* The thinking type wants to know, "Is it *right?*" "Does it make *logical sense?*" These are the key questions a thinker will consider when making a decision or sorting out the world. The person with a strong thinking preference often tends to state their positions bluntly and their decisions are often impersonal and do not always pay attention to the wishes of others. They are the least flexible of all types in their ideas.

The person who prefers thinking has several traits that are likely to get them in trouble when they are outside of an environment dominated by other thinkers. For one thing, they have a *critiquing mind.* When interacting with others, they tend to begin by believing others are wrong. They need to have others prove their ideas logically and orderly before they will believe them.

They also see "critique" as discussion. When they criticize someone, they don't intend their criticism in a personal way. For the thinker, their criticism is simply a candid, normal discussion and they are likely to be surprised when someone is hurt.

This is compounded by the thinking characteristic of often coming across as brief and quite businesslike. They can appear to be lacking in gentleness and compassion.

The Thinking Function in Scripture

We find many instances of Jesus's use of his thinking function. When Jesus clears out the temple (Matthew 21:12–17), this function is operational. We notice how Jesus comes directly to the point in a very blunt and clear way. He is acting on what he believes is just and right in the situation with which he is faced. He is not necessarily concerned with harmony and getting along with others in this case, but is more concerned with the obvious breach of justice and truth.

When Jesus tells the disciples to "shake the dust from your feet" (Matthew 10:14), he is also operating from his thinking function. Jesus shows an assertiveness with his words. He shows a firmness, a clear decisive approach to the situation at hand as he sends his disciples off on a new venture.

A classic "thinking line" from scripture is found in Matthew's account of Jesus's Sermon on the Mount, where Jesus says, "All you need say is 'Yes' if you mean yes, 'No' if you mean no; anything more than this comes from the Evil One" (5:37). This is a fine example of his preference for thinking. Jesus does not mince words. He is direct and to the point and urges others to be the same.

The psalmists speak many times of Yahweh, our God of *power and might.* Psalm 89 states: "Yours is a strong arm, mighty your hand, your right hand raised high; Saving Justice and Fair Judgment the foundations of your throne, Faithful Love and Constancy march before you." This Justice and Judgment are surely thinking characteristics.

In our Church's history we can look back to many of the saints and see how they show us characteristics of the thinking function. St. Thomas Aquinas was a man who was very analytical in his thinking process and who became a great Doctor of the Church.

The Feeling Function

Let's take a look at the other 50 percent of the U.S. population who make their decisions using the feeling function (represented by the letter "F"). In acting upon their environment, feeling types prefer to use more *personal* value systems to think through to conclusions. Among the values they will use are sentiment, relationships, and harmony.

They seem to be able to place themselves in others' shoes and show sympathy and compassion. Feeling types are more apt to enjoy working in areas of counseling, ministry, and social service than their thinking counterparts, as they relate well to most people and can evaluate situations in terms of what is best for people. The feeler often appears as a tender, personal, and compassionate person. Their deep need is to live in *harmony* with others and the environment. They also desire intimacy with others and will often become a close friend.

They may dislike telling people unpleasant things and may avoid touchy subjects. Feeling individuals are the people in a group who will quickly try to change the subject when a conflict arises. They may have difficulty correcting others. In many prayer groups and religious communities with which we have worked, we often find feeling-type leaders who will avoid direct confrontations with those who should be corrected, and will, instead, give a "teaching" or "chapter" to the whole group and hope the individuals will hear the message and correct their ways. Confrontation can be a very traumatic experience for the feeling type, especially if they are also introverted.

Jesus's Use of Feeling

As we look at Jesus in the scriptures, we find one who heals the wounded, the lame, and the sick. Jesus stresses forgiveness and compassion to sinners, as he did with the sinner woman who wept at his feet and anointed and kissed them (Luke 7:36–50). We see Jesus acting out of love and sympathy for his friend Lazarus as Jesus wept and called out to the Father before Lazarus was raised from the dead (John 11:1–44).

Jesus shows us his intimacy with the Father and how he desires that same intimacy among his followers when he prays, "May they all be one, just as, Father, you are in me and I am in you, so that they also may be in us, so that the world may believe it was you who sent me. I have given them the glory you gave to me, that they may be one as we are one" (John 17:21–22).

In the apostle Peter we see the feeling preference. When Jesus asks him, "Do you love me?" he answers, "Yes, Lord, you know I love you" (John 21:15–17). Elsewhere Jesus asks the disciples, "Who do you say I am?" Then Peter answers, "You are the Christ, the Son of the living God" (Matthew 16:13–16). These scriptures portray Peter as one who is intimate with Jesus, speaks to him on a personal level, and is able to express his emotions and thoughts to him.

Contrasts Between Thinking and Feeling

The thinker is concerned with objective facts while the feeling type is concerned with more subjective circumstances. If, for example, a problem is at hand such as dealing with the discipline of a child, the thinker may be more concerned with the objective facts. How exactly has the child misbehaved? Given the same circumstances, a feeling-type individual may want to know the subjective circumstances. They may want to know about what led up to the misbehavior and to be aware of the child's feelings about the situation.

The feeler will try to persuade others to accept their decision and might be more open to negotiation and compromise, while the thinker will tend to be more rigid.

The thinker will focus on justice and what they believe to be right, while the feeler will want to do what they think is more humane and will produce the most harmonious outcome.

The thinker tends to be better equipped to critique an idea and look at it logically and analytically. The feeler will be more appreciative of an idea and of valuing the persons involved or the originator.

"Intelligence" and "Emotions"

We spoke earlier of the mistaken notion that the thinking function dealt with intelligence and the feeling function dealt with emotions. First we want to reiterate that neither type has any advantage or disadvantage in either intelligence or emotions. The preferred decision-making function has nothing to do with brain power. When it comes to IQ, there is virtually no evidence of IQ being tied to the thinking/feeling preference. We mentioned, too, that the feeling type has no monopoly on emotions. Both these types experience the full range of emotions. The fact that the feeling type makes decisions based on harmony would suggest that feelings play a stronger role in their decisions. However, this could not and should not be understood as emotional decisions.

Rational and Irrational

The mistaken notion that feeling individuals make decisions based on "feelings," and thus "emotions," and that thinkers make decisions based on logic, leads to the mistaken conclusion that thinking is the "rational" function and feeling is the "irrational" function. This is simply not so. Jung characterized *both* thinking and feeling as the *rational* functions. They are rational because they are used to act upon the world, and they require conscious action by the individual. Sensing and intuiting are the *irrational* functions, since they are performed more passively. They are the functions by which we *perceive* the world. We "irrationally" stand by as the world comes to us. The thinking/feeling preference requires our rational action. Thus, Jung saw neither thinking nor feeling as emotional or irrational.

QUESTIONS FOR REFLECTION

1. Based on the descriptions of thinking and feeling, what is your preference and how strong is that preference in your personality?

2. What are the main characteristics of this type that lead you to make this choice?

3. What do you think is the function, thinking or feeling, of the person closest to you? (spouse, friend, close relative, etc.)

4. What was a situation in which both your and this person's preferences were evident?

5. Think of an important decision you recently made. Was your conclusion based more on harmony and relationships or on truth and logic? Explain.

5

The Attitudes of Judging and Perceiving

This final set of attitudes was not an explicit part of Jung's theory but was nonetheless implied, and it was formally added by the Myers-Briggs team. It has to do with our preference for acting upon our environment or waiting for our environment to act upon us. When dealing with the *outside world*, each of us prefers either to use our judging functions (thinking or feeling) to *make decisions*, or to use our perceiving functions (sensing or intuiting) and *leave our options open*.

Just as with the previous characteristics, we are all blends of both judging and perceiving. None of us is "pure." But, just as we prefer either the right hand or the left, we prefer either judging or perceiving. Also, they are both good. Both are made in the image and likeness of God, and Jesus shows us both preferences.

Judging

The first term, "judging" or "J", is one that often carries a negative connotation. It is, perhaps, a poor choice, but it is, nevertheless, descriptive. It should not be confused with the more negative term "judgmental"; both judgers and perceivers can be "judgmental."

Those who prefer judging make up about 50 percent of the U.S. population and they are those who like to get things decided and finished. They do not like open options. They prefer to have decisions behind them rather than ahead of them. These are people who prefer to "act upon their environment." They are decisive and they like to reach closure on the open issues of their lives. They tend to live according to plans, and they are not especially thrilled by having the unexpected sprung on them.

The person who prefers judging will likely be the organized, exacting, and self-regimented type. We mentioned in chapter 3 that sensing types are usually the ones with the organized spice racks and all their tools hanging on Peg-Boards. The judging type who prefers sensing has arranged the spices in *alphabetical order* and probably has *outlined* all their tools on their Peg-Board!

As you will see, the attitude of judging is directly connected with the "judging" functions of thinking and feeling. When we employ this judging or decision-making attitude, we do so by means of either our thinking or our feeling function, as this is the function we use to "act upon our environment."

Perceiving

The other half of the population, those who engage in perceiving, or "P", are those who let the environment act upon them. While, as we have said, judgers see life as something to be acted upon, perceivers see life as something to be experienced.

Perceivers like to wait for things to happen. They are the curious types who prefer to keep their options open. They tend to be much more spontaneous and can more easily "roll with the punches." These folks will often wait until the last minute to make decisions and thus are often accused of being procrastinators. The main concern of the perceiver is to have enough information before making a decision. Their aim is to miss nothing. And they like to see what will happen. As a result, they can be flexible, adaptable, and often open-minded. A tight schedule can make a perceiver feel stifled. They prefer flexibility and they may love surprises and the unexpected.

Just as the judging attitude is connected to the thinking/

feeling functions, the perceiving attitude is connected to the sensing/intuiting functions. When we are "letting the world come to us," which is the perceiver's attitude toward life, we do so by use of either our sensing function or our intuiting function.

In a close relationship, perceivers and judgers will usually react differently to the same set of circumstances. The judgers will prefer some sort of schedule for meals, work, and recreation and have a good idea how their day will unfold. They like to plan ahead. Perceivers will prefer to live a more flexible day. They will more likely eat when they are hungry, work when something demands their attention, and play when the opportunity arises.

The best scripture example of this contrasting approach is the story of Martha and Mary (Luke 10:38–42). Martha wanted to take care of the scheduled jobs that needed tending, while Mary had a more interesting diversion at the moment—Jesus. Martha and Mary are excellent examples of this pair of attitudes.

Contrast of the Two Attitudes

Judgers want things settled, while perceivers prefer open options and would rather not be confined to making a decision quickly.

Perceivers like to plan "on the run," while judgers tend to plan ahead.

Judgers see circumstances in terms of the "end," and consequently completed, while perceivers see an event as something "yet to happen."

Perceivers are not as affected by schedules and deadlines, while judgers have more a sense of urgency.

Judgers tend to believe they know what others should do, while perceivers are more aware of what others are doing and are anxious to see the outcome.

Jesus's Use of Judging and Perceiving

Jesus's life shows us both attitudes. In the story of the adulterous woman (John 8:3–11), when the woman was brought before him, he waited. He did not use any words. He simply
leaned over and started writing on the ground with his finger.
Then the scribes and the Pharisees persisted in questioning
Jesus. Only then did he say, "Let the one among you who is
guiltless be the first to throw a stone at her" (8:7). Then he
bent down and wrote on the ground again. There was no sense
of urgency. There was a flexibility in his manner as he allowed
the situation to unfold.

At other times, we see Jesus as he acts upon the environment. When the disciple turned away the little children (Matthew 19:13–15), Jesus said, "Let the little children alone, and
do not stop them from coming to me . . ." He was oriented
toward a goal. Then he laid his hands on them and continued
on his way. He had a plan and followed it through.

Attitudes and Functions

As we addressed the four pairs of preferences, we spoke of
"attitudes" and "functions." We said that introvert/extravert
and judging/perceiving were pairs of "attitudes." We also described sensing/intuiting and thinking/feeling as pairs of
"functions." For the sake of our "primer," let it suffice to say
that attitudes describe ways we use the functions. The "functions" (S/N, T/F) can be said to be the essence of our personality, while the "attitudes" (I/E, J/P) describe the style we use
to present the functions to the world.

Judging and perceiving can be said to be "generic" and
denote which function an individual prefers to use ex-
travertedly, in the *outer world*, that is, either their "specific"
judging function, thinking or feeling, or their "specific" perceiving function, sensing or intuiting.

The introvert/extravert preferences tell us the world in
which we prefer to live, that is, the inner or introverted world
or the outer or extraverted world.

QUESTIONS FOR REFLECTION

1. Based on the descriptions of judging and perceiving, what is your preference and how strong is that preference in your personality?

2. What are the main characteristics of this type that lead you to make this choice?

3. What do you think is the attitude, judging or perceiving, of the person closest to you? (spouse, friend, close relative, etc.)

4. What was a situation in which both your and this person's preferences were evident?

5. Do you prefer having decisions made and sticking with them, or leaving options open to see what unfolds? Explain.

6

Determining Your Type

The information we have just reviewed and the further details that will follow are of little value if they are not applied to ourself and our personality. We can only do that if we take the time to identify our own personality type using this format. This process is accomplished ideally with the aid of a completed Myers-Briggs Type Indicator and a qualified MBTI consultant. However, the process can also be done without the benefit of the instrument if we are willing to spend some time looking at type descriptions and our own behavior.

Those who have taken the MBTI could take the position that they have the results of their Myers-Briggs, thus their type must be the result provided by the instrument. We cannot be quite that rigid. The MBTI does not determine our type. We are each responsible for determining our own type. The MBTI is only a tool that helps us begin the process.

For many, the MBTI results will identify their type accurately. Statistically, the tool is 80–85 percent accurate. So for 80–85 percent of us, there will be no need to look further than the type shown on the MBTI. However, even for those whose results are accurate, it is vitally important that the process we outline below be experienced to allow "ownership" of our type.

If we are unwilling to work on identifying our own type, the material in the chapters which follow may cause uncertainty. It is one thing to learn about Typology, it is quite another to apply its values to our own life and situation. This book is intended for this latter purpose. As we move through the growth and development theories of Typology, we will speak of those who are feeling types, thinking types, etc. There will be less value if you are not endeavoring to identify your own type.

"Reaching Closure" Can Be Difficult

Whether we have access to Myers-Briggs results or are going it alone, reaching "closure," that is deciding on our type, can be a difficult process. There are a number of reasons for this. First and foremost is a fact which we mentioned often in the previous chapters. We are all blends of each characteristic. None of us is pure. It is quite easy to see some of each type in our behavior. This is a valid observation, and for some people it is more true than for others.

This is further complicated by a tendency we all seem to have in being preoccupied with the desire to appear and believe we are "totally balanced" and well integrated. At times we avoid seeing ourselves as one-sided or preferring one behavior over another. We often want to believe that our growth is behind us and now we have it all together. The idea of not having total freedom is an idea we naturally resist. It sounds somehow sinful to us. The truth is, Jesus showed us the perfect freedom in his life as seen in the Gospels. None of us has or will reach that same level of freedom. We all have growth ahead of us, as that seems to be part of the human condition.

None of us is totally balanced. We all have preferred behavior. We all use either our right hand or our left hand a little better than the other. None of us is perfectly ambidextrous. So too with our behavior. All four pairs of these characteristics are opposites. We cannot use the two parts of any pair at the same time. Thus, over time, we do prefer to choose one over the other. Naturally. We are not speaking of the ability to choose behavior opposite of our preference when it is appropriate. Each of us has *some* degree of freedom to choose our actions, and we will discuss this later. But on the natural level, without choosing, we will each prefer one characteristic from each pair over its opposite.

A friend of ours described preference as walking into an ice cream shop that only carries vanilla and chocolate. (No vanilla-fudge!) Each of us will have a natural preference to choose either vanilla or chocolate. Not that we cannot and sometimes do choose the opposite, but we will spontaneously, naturally choose one more often than the other. So too with introvert/ extravert, thinking/feeling, etc.

Another reason that determining our type is difficult is that we often behave differently in different roles. That is, we might be one personality type as a worker, another as a church leader, another as a parent, another as a spouse. While it is unlikely we will be a wide range of types, it is not uncommon for us to behave as more than one, depending on the expecta-tions of our roles. We meet many persons in business who are called to exhibit very specific thinking behavior while they are at work, but when they come home they are different people, as they are free to behave more naturally. While we *can* utilize the opposite functions when required, the characteristics that are not our preferred behavior will cost more energy. As they are not naturally within our "comfort zone" it takes more effort to sustain such unnatural behavior.

Whether I am attempting to guess my type or answer a series of questions on the Myers-Briggs Type Indicator, the issue becomes: What "hat" was I wearing when I guessed my type or answered the MBTI questions? If I was wearing my "work hat," then my guess or MBTI results will indicate my work personality type. If I was wearing my "religious church leader hat," then the answer will produce that personality type. An-swered in this way, none of these resultant personalities will be our most natural, spontaneous self.

This is the reason one should answer the MBTI questions as if they were at home with their shoes off. Answers should not be as we would like to behave, or think we should behave. Nor should we give answers we think would be more Christian or what others would like better. Rather, we should answer the questions and guess the type that best describes our natural and spontaneous preference.

If you are attempting to determine your type without the benefit of the MBTI, try to follow these same cautions.

It is usually about this time that the question comes up: Are these characteristics caused by heredity, or by the environment? Were we born with these preferences, or did our childhood environment cause them to be formed? The answer seems to be both.

Actually, there is no definite answer. Various Myers-Briggs practitioners will give different answers. Some believe that the personality traits are hereditary and others believe they are caused by our environment. Some characteristics can be seen at very early ages.

For example, it is often quite easy to determine if a young child is an introvert or extravert. We often see an extraverted child who is always focused outside of his or her own little world. They constantly seek attention and want to be around other children. They seem to seek involvement with their outer world of people, places, and things.

The introverted child, on the other hand, is content to be alone. They will more comfortably be at home in their own company, content to look through books and play happily with their toys. The introverted child is the child who could be put in a sandbox alone and would be content for longer periods of time than an extraverted youngster.

The other characteristics are less obvious in young children, and either the hereditary or environmental explanation seems plausible to us. Using either theory, the personality type seems to be well entrenched by the time we reach about seven years old.

Responsibility

Unlike some "tests," the MBTI does not impose a type or description upon you as it is not a test but an indicator. You are the final judge of your type. As we've mentioned, the MBTI is a tool to start that process. Only you can agree or disagree with the results.

Try to choose the behavior that best describes how you actually behave. Even if you would like to make decisions based on the feeling function, if you usually end up deciding based on the facts and logic, then you are likely a thinker, as this describes the way you usually behave. Further, all the types are good, there is no right or wrong type. They are all made in God's image.

MBTI Results

If you have taken the MBTI, depending on the form, you answered from 50 to 290 questions. The common element of each of the forms is that the scoring produces a four-letter result. The indicator will pick one type from each pair. Either E or I, S or N, etc. This will produce a four-letter composite such as INFJ, ESTP, etc. The letters are always presented in the same order we presented the characteristics in chapters 2 through 5. I/E, followed by S/N, then T/F, and finally J/P). There are sixteen types in all (four times four).

While the MBTI is 80 to 85 percent accurate (the fifty-question abbreviated form is less accurate), many people still have to look further than the indicator itself, and the clarification could be on any of the four pairs. It is also important to note that completing the MBTI during a period of crisis or while experiencing change or stress can result in significantly inaccurate results.

Numbers

In addition to the letter identification, the MBTI produces several sets of numbers. If you receive the actual answer sheet back with your results, you will see a box in one corner which looks like this (the format is different on the abbreviated form):

```
┌─────────────────────────────────────┐
│           POINTS      SCORES         │
│                                      │
│   E _____ I _____   _____         │
│                                      │
│   S _____ N _____   _____         │
│                                      │
│   T _____ F _____   _____         │
│                                      │
│   J _____ P _____   _____         │
│                                      │
│   TYPE                               │
│                                      │
└─────────────────────────────────────┘
```

Usually, the first set of numbers are labeled "points." Please ignore this column for now. They are the raw numbers produced by the answers from which are derived the more important "scores."

The scores are the second set of numbers, usually following or below the letters. These numbers denote the statistical *strength* of each preference. Here again, we will cover these numbers in more detail later, but for now they are of help in reaching closure on your own type. The "scores" denote the strength of your preference for introversion, sensing, etc.

The MBTI process will produce no "zero" scores and only odd numbers: 1, 3, 5, etc. A single digit score (up to 9) denotes a low preference strength. Don't apply judgment to this! This has nothing to do with good or bad, only the strength of the preference. If numbers are low, it simply means that, had a few questions been answered differently, you might have scored the opposite preference. Thus, a low score is a "red flag" that tells us we may have to look closer at a pair of functions or attitudes.

The first step to determining your type is to decide which type you will use for your starting point. If you are doing this without benefit of an MBTI, then go back to the "guesses" you made at the end of chapters 2–5 and compile your best guess of your type. (If you didn't do it then, it would be well to do so now.) If you have the MBTI results, start with the type identified by the instrument.

Sketches

The Appendix at the end of this book contains a brief sketch for each of the sixteen types. The sketches are descriptions of typical behavior of the types. Other sketches or profiles have been written and we recommend you use as many resources in this area as possible. Extensive profiles can be found in *Please Understand Me*[1] and the booklet "Introduction to Type."[2]

Though no sketch is perfect, studying them can be the key to determining your type. As you read the sketches, you will find that some characteristics agree with your behavior while others do not. Some of the examples will prove relevant, others will not. There is an often-used Typology axiom that says, *"All* INFJ's are like *all other* INFJ's, are like *some other* INFJ's, are like *no other* INFJ's."* (It does make sense and it applies to all sixteen types!) In other words, people of the same personality type have many things in common, but they are also unique. For this reason, you will agree with some of the descriptions in the sketches, but not necessarily all of them.

Reaching Closure

As you read the sketch of the personality type you guessed or the one shown on the MBTI, do so with a pen or pencil in hand and underline the characteristics that seem to accurately describe you. Put a question mark in the margin of those items which you do not see in yourself. After you've read the sketch, ask yourself, "How does it fit overall?" Perhaps it fits like a glove. If it does, great! The process of determining our type ends when we find the type description that best describes our behavior.

Adjustments

What if the sketch doesn't exactly fit? Perhaps there are parts that are accurate, but other, significant descriptions that are not accurate. First, look at the characteristics with which you disagree. If they are simply examples of behavior, then perhaps those examples should be ignored. But, if there are aspects of the type that simply don't describe how you behave, we can use one of the benefits of Typology, that is, the ability to adjust the sketch until we find a good fit.

If you have the Myers-Briggs results, look at the scores. Choose the characteristic which scored the lowest preference strength and read the sketch with that preference reversed. For example, if the sketch that didn't seem to fit is INF*P,* and the score of the "P" was 3, you should read the sketch with the J/P reversed. Thus, the INF*J* sketch might prove to describe your behavior better. If you are guessing your type without benefit of the MBTI, for adjustment go first to the pair of functions or attitudes you had most difficulty guessing, the ones that seemed unclear to you. Here again, read the type with that pair reversed.

What if you have the MBTI and had two low scores? Look at the guesses you made as you went through chapters 2 through 5. Choose the next sketches to read based on the combination of low scores *and* those you guessed opposite.

Another way to help determine your type is to have your spouse or a close friend read the sketches and help you. Ask them to go through the sketch with pencil in hand and highlight those areas that are very much like you or that are not at all like you. Still, you are the final judge. No one can decide your type for you.

There is a risk when individuals participate in a workshop and then attempt to tell other people their type. Guessing another's type is very risky business. We have seen couples married fifty years who are unable to guess their spouse's type. There are many reasons for this, including misunderstandings of the type descriptions. Often we misguess our own type and another's because we don't fully understand the pairs of characteristics. We sometimes latch on to one example of the behavior of a type and conclude that characteristic is the most significant description of the type while there may be a number of more significant factors.

Remember, Typology is not meant to box you in. The objective of this process is to find the personality type that best describes your behavior. It's important that you be honest with yourself. You are trying to select the type that best describes how you actually behave, not how you would like to behave, or how you would like others to see you. You need to ask which sketch describes your behavior best.

Determining our type is a crucial part of the process of applying Typology to our own life and relationships. We urge you to try to "come to closure" on your own type before you move on. However, if you are unable to do so, feel free to proceed with an eye toward reaching that conclusion as you continue. For some, the chapters ahead will clarify your understanding of the type characteristics, while for others, integrating a subject such as this simply takes more time.

REFLECTION QUESTIONS

1. What is your personality type based on your original guesses?

2. What is your personality type based on the MBTI results, if available?

3. After reading the appropriate sketches, which best describes you?

4. What are the most accurate points in this sketch?

5. Did you learn anything new about yourself? What?

NOTES

1. David Keirsey and Marilyn Bates, *Please Understand Me* (Del Mar, Calif.: Prometheus Nemesis Books, 1984), Appendix.

2. Isabel Briggs Myers (Palo Alto, Calif.: Consulting Psychologists Press, 1962).

PART II

The Value
of
Typology

7

The Value of Typology to Individuals

Typology can have tremendous value in the many facets of our lives. The first value, and addressed in this chapter, is the value Typology has to each of us as *individuals*, in knowledge of ourself and our spiritual journey. The next two areas of value, and covered in the next two chapters, are to us as spouses, friends, and parents and, finally, the value to us in community situations, be they secular or religious, related to work, worship, or living situations.

We need to know who we are and how God has made us. We each have a unique set of fingerprints; no two in this world are exactly alike. God has given us each quite different personalities, as well as our individual physical qualities. We each react to circumstances in different ways. Each of us has different emotions and feelings when placed in a similar set of circumstances. God calls each of us into a relationship with himself. He uses the type of personality he has given us and the circumstances in which we live to give us a message. Each of our journeys will be somewhat unique.

As we grow in understanding and acceptance of how he has made us, we will gain a more wholesome love of ourself. This helps us to realize that we should not struggle to be like anyone else. This self-acceptance is the essential ingredient in our truly loving God and those people who are a part of our life.

The Conscious

To better understand the value of Typology, it is quite helpful to understand the concepts of the conscious and the unconscious that we spoke of in chapter 1 and to take them a little further. Let us briefly look at the idea of the conscious. Nearly all psychological theories agree that there are two parts to our makeup. One is our conscious self, the part of the reality that we mentioned in chapter 1 and whose center is our ego. It is the part of ourselves of which we are currently *aware*. If you are sitting somewhere now reading this book, you are "aware" of certain aspects of your own identity, such as being a man or a woman, that you are alone or with others. You are aware of your physical surroundings and if you are hot or cold, comfortable or uncomfortable. You are aware of your present thoughts and feelings. Along with much more, the conscious also contains your strong personality traits, your viewpoints and values at a given moment.

In summary, the conscious contains only those parts of ourself of which we are *currently aware,* and is believed to be only about 10 percent of our total being. As mentioned before, the center of this conscious part of ourselves is known as the ego. This ego—which is Latin for "I"—directs our conscious life. It is the controlling factor of our consciousness. In the context we are speaking of, it is important that it be strong and well developed. Failure to have a well-developed ego results in being tossed about in everyday life situations.

The Unconscious

Carl Jung maintained that there is far more to our psychological makeup than that of which we are aware. This leads us to the 90 percent that is our unconscious. A great deal of our behavior and decisions come from this *hidden* part of ourselves known as the *unconscious.* This is the part of which our conscious self, or ego, is unaware. It is naive to believe that, just because we are unaware of this part of ourself, it has no effect on our behavior. This was the "hidden self" that St. Paul prayed should grow strong in his letter to the Ephesians (3:16).

Each of us has a vast reservoir of information which is beyond that of which we are conscious. Some of it can become available to us, but at any given moment most of it is hidden. The unconscious holds a universe of unseen energies and forces. It is the secret source of many of our thoughts, feelings, and behavior.

Jung maintains that this unconscious (or non-conscious) is made up of two parts: the personal and the collective.

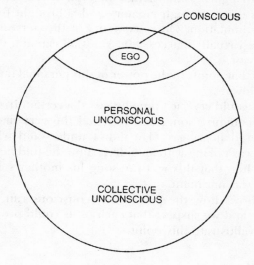

THE TOTAL BEING

The Personal Unconscious

The personal unconscious is that part of our hidden self that we have acquired because of our own personal experiences. It contains all of our unique memories. It is made up of everything that has passed through our conscious because of our individual life experience. It is unique to us.

Our personal unconscious contains all of our formerly perceived reality. All of the memories from our childhood are stored there. All of our many (forgotten) interactions with our parents, other relatives, and friends, the times we felt loved and unloved, or passed over. All of our education and schooling and the things we have learned in our past experiences are stored away in this vast reservoir. The personal unconscious contains the emotions we have experienced throughout our life: joy, sorrow, pain . . .

All of this material is still there within the recesses of our minds, residing in our unconscious, stored away until it is brought to light. Some of this material is accessible to our conscious mind through memory and is brought forth by all sorts of stimulation. Other contents of the personal unconscious are virtually inaccessible. Yet it all can and does affect our behavior.

A story that points to the power of this personal unconscious is the following:

A man would cry each time he heard a certain Irish song. It wasn't a common song, and he cried the very first time he remembered hearing it. He didn't understand why. Once, when he was talking with an elderly aunt, he told her about it. She told him that this was the song his mother sang to him when he was an infant.

This shows how the personal unconscious can affect our behavior, and we suspect that each of us could provide more stories to illustrate this point.

The Collective Unconscious

The other part of this vast unconscious reservoir is the collective unconscious. This is the part that "came with the package" when we were born. This is the aspect of our identity that God gives to all human beings. The easiest to understand are our instincts. For example, no one has to teach an infant to nurse; the instinct is just "there." So too with most of the others. But it doesn't end there. Jung did extensive studies to determine other types of material with which we are born, and he made some fascinating discoveries.

Jung learned that throughout the ages humans have had

many symbols in common with one another that were not taught. The essence of a symbol is always deeper than its obvious, surface meaning. Its origin is buried in the past and throughout many cultures. For example, in nearly all cultures the symbol of "light" seems to represent knowledge and good. The contrasting symbol of "darkness" represents fear, evil, and the unknown. So too, the symbol of water in many cultures suggests new life and cleansing. In addition, Jung spent years researching certain other "universal" symbols, which he called archetypes. For those who wish a greater understanding of this important concept, we recommend Jung's book *Man and His Symbols.* [1]

Since there is so much hidden within each of us, both personal *and* collective, it is important that we recognize the effect this material has upon the way we behave. St. Paul speaks of that inner struggle when he says, "I do not understand my own behavior; I do not act as I mean to, but I do things that I hate" (Romans 7:15).

Perhaps you have had a time in your life when you experienced an emotion that was out of proportion to the circumstances. Maybe someone was critical or said that you could have handled a situation differently and you blew up, got very angry, vehemently disagreed, and said some things that you wish you hadn't and then wondered where all of that energy came from. This could be an example of finding ourself doing the very things we hate.

As Robert Johnson states in his book *Inner Work:* "Jung showed that the unconscious is the creative source of all that evolves into the conscious mind and into the total personality of each individual. It is out of the raw material of the unconscious that our conscious minds develop, mature, and expand to include all the qualities that we carry potentially within us. It is from this treasure trove that we are enriched with strengths and qualities we never knew we possessed." [2]

The treasure of understanding this concept is that the more we understand this hidden part of ourselves, the less likely it is to "take over" our behavior. The first step to the freedom which is being offered here, the freedom to choose our own behavior, is to understand that hidden part of our personality.

Once we understand some of that hidden part, we gain the knowledge we need to move forward. As we slowly grow in understanding bits and pieces of our unconscious and integrate them into our conscious life, our control over our own behavior increases and is strengthened.

Understanding Typology is a healthy and positive beginning to the inner journey and to a better understanding of this complex being that God has created.

We said that understanding the hidden self is the first step. It is not the "final" step. As we grow in understanding, we have the potential to make more conscious decisions about our behavior. It is this freedom that can allow us truly to begin to apply Jesus's values.

Suppose our natural preference is to make decisions using our feeling function rather than our thinking function. Further, suppose we are now in the position of being a leader in a group. Tom, a member of the group, is disturbing the meetings. He takes up everyone's attention and energy, bringing up all his personal problems, which seem endless. Whatever the topic being discussed, Tom brings the focus back to himself. Our preference for using our feeling function is strong, and we see that in this particular situation we will need to call upon our thinking function. We know we will need to be assertive and to confront Tom about his behavior. Discipline and confrontation are extremely difficult in this case, and we spend a great amount of energy trying to think of another solution. Deep down inside, we know that the right thing to do is to talk openly with Tom. How will we handle it?

We can desperately want to do the right thing, but if we do not have the *freedom to choose* the appropriate behavior, all of our "wanting" is in vain.

We have in Typology a tool to help us to understand ourself. Its use can be the beginning of the road to the inner journey of the soul. Typology can help us to accept and love ourself and our neighbors and thus to accept and to love God. We can begin to understand our behavior. We can see that we are made in God's image and we share these traits with his incarnate Son.

We have a tool to see our strengths and also our weaknesses.

Typology can be an invitation to us to explore that inner world of the unconscious with which God has blessed us. It can be the gateway that can lead us to an ever deeper exploring of our full potential as a child of God. Some other areas to which this exploration may take us is seeing what our dreams have to tell us and using our imagination in prayer.

On our journey to God, there are many paths, many roads. Typology can help us on that journey. Through it, we may come to a deeper acceptance of our self identity and we may grow in intimacy and the awareness of how very much God loves us. As we accept that gift of our humanity we are, in a sense, giving glory to God who created us. We are acknowledging that he didn't make a mistake when he made us, that he truly knew us before all time, that he loved us into being and knit us together in our mother's womb (Psalm 139). Perhaps we can rejoice that, when we were born, he looked, smiled, and said, "You are exactly what I wanted. You are exactly what I had in mind."

As we are better able to accept ourself, we are better able to accept God's love. In receiving that great gift of his love at the very core and center of our being, we are better able to share that love in our acceptance of and response to the other human beings he has placed in our life, even though those persons are different, and those differences can cause conflict.

The more deeply rooted we are in the love and acceptance of God and ourself, with all of our strengths and weaknesses, the more freedom we have to love those he has placed on our road of life.

Seeing Limitations as Gifts

Each of us has areas of giftedness and strength in our personality. It is indeed a grace to be in touch with those parts of ourself. We also have areas about which we have many doubts and apprehensions, parts of ourself of which we are not especially fond or proud. Areas of selfishness or fear or pride. But these are also parts of our humanity. To accept both our giftedness and our limitations is the beginning of growth and maturity.

Part of our growth may be to change our attitude concerning our limitations. We may need to see them as *gifts*. In fact, the things we *cannot* do are just as much a part of our giftedness as the things we *can* do.

There are three primary benefits in recognizing our limitations. First, they point to our finiteness. If we become aware of our limitations, we may see that we cannot do everything. We may recognize that we are weak and broken, and we may become more accepting of others' limitations. This discovery can lead us to the second and third values of recognizing our limitations.

Our limitations help us to recognize our need for others. They make us more dependent. This puts us in the posture of receiver, of one who needs help. We need to depend on one another, upon the community, the Body of Christ. As St. Paul states in his letter to the Romans: "Just as each of us has various parts in one body, and the parts do not all have the same function: in the same way, all of us, though there are so many of us, make up one body in Christ, and as different parts we are all joined to one another . . . the gifts that we have differ according to the grace that was given to each of us" (Romans 12:4–6).

All of us are gifted in various ways. Not one of us can do everything. God does not expect us to do everything that needs doing in our church, or to be everything for everyone who has a need. When we accept and recognize this, we are able to rely on one another. We are able to depend on other people to use their special gifts.

We need one another. We must rely and depend on one another. Not one of us is capable of being all the parts of the body. And this openness leads us to the final value:

Our limitations point us to our need for God. Our very brokenness requires dependence, and only in our consent to receive God's grace can he work, as in Mary's attitude at the time of the Annunciation: "You see before you the Lord's servant, let it happen to me as you have said" (Luke 1:38). As long as we believe we can "do it all," God cannot be our strength.

Our suggestion for bringing about this growth is to study

and to pray. Study the qualities that are explained for your type, both the sketch for your unique type found in the Appendix and the descriptions of the individual characteristics in chapters 2–5. Learn more about your qualities. Pray and work to accept them, embrace them, own them, and develop them. Become skilled in using them. If you are an "ISTP," be the *best* "ISTP" that you can. In your prayer, ask God for the grace to be everything he wants you to be.

Then study and pray about the other qualities, the ones that are not your natural gifts. Begin to see the value and beauty in them as well. Recognize that they too reside within you; that they too are good and in God's image. Pray for the grace to accept them as well, to embrace them, to own them, and, as we'll see in chapter 10, to develop them.

Let us continue on this journey on which we have embarked. Let us continue to speak of and seek the supreme gift of the Father: *freedom.*

QUESTIONS FOR REFLECTION

1. As you reflect on this material, where do you see the most potential for value in your own personal growth?

2. What is an occasion or circumstance when material from your unconscious affected your behavior? How?

3. What characteristics and qualities of your type do you most accept and value? Why?

4. What characteristics and qualities of your type do you least accept and value? Why?

NOTES

1. Carl G. Jung, *Man and His Symbols* (Garden City, N.Y.: Doubleday & Company, 1964).

2. Robert A. Johnson, *Inner Work* (San Francisco: Harper & Row, 1986), page 6.

8

The Value of Typology to the Couple and the Family

While the topic of this chapter seems limited to the married couple and the family unit, we wish to expand the application to the unmarried as well. Many, by circumstance or choice, are not in a marriage relationship. However, many are involved in a healthy close personal relationship with another person and it is in that special relationship that much of the value we see to the married couple can also be applied. So we invite those unmarried readers to approach this chapter from that perspective.

If we are married and truly see our marriage as a sacrament, a *sign* of Christ's presence in the world, we will continually strive to grow in wholeness and holiness both individually and as a couple and to welcome and accept Jesus's call to be united in our love. This is both a joy and a challenge in our marriage. Our relationship is fragile and delicate. Our life together, with its many deaths and risings, can bring new hope to our everyday life.

Opposites Attract

Both experience and research has proved that we are often attracted to a person with a personality opposite to ours. Jung maintains, for many reasons, that opposites even fascinate one another. This seeming natural "instinct" holds true for those we choose as close friends and those we tend to marry, and there are many theories about why this is so often the case. Most of us can see this lived out in our own lives or in that of others, such as our parents.

The studies which have been done using Typology as a foundation tell us that the "average" married couple has two of the characteristics in common (such as being an introvert or a thinker) and two that are opposite (one a senser, the other an intuitive, etc.).

The shared characteristic allows the couple to have common interests and the opposite characteristic is what makes things "interesting." We can be drawn to a partner with characteristics either like our own or opposite of our own. The latter may be an unconscious effort to complete parts of ourself that are lacking. For example, a very extraverted, thinking person might be drawn to marry a quiet, more sensitive, introverted feeling person. Such a person may unconsciously feel that those characteristics are becoming a part of themselves. Of course, the introverted feeling type is drawn to the other for the same reason.

These are the precise characteristics in our own marriage—although in our travels we have seen many couples with all four characteristics exactly the same, as well as all four opposite.

Studies have been done on the effect of type similarity or difference in marriages that are "happy" or "unhappy" or functional or dysfunctional. Based on questions about longevity of marriage, and the degree of happiness the partners expressed with their marriage, the research indicates that, regardless of the type similarities or differences, all couples have the same *potential* for marital happiness (or unhappiness). That is, a couple with all four characteristics the same is just as apt to consider themselves happily married as a couple with all four characteristics opposite. (We would maintain that life might be a lot more interesting for this latter couple.)

Differences Can Be Helpful

The type differences we bring to our marriages or close relationships—be they an opposite preference or variant degrees in the strength of our shared preferences—can be valuable and helpful. We can often complement one another and bring a sense of wholeness to our relationship that each individual on his or her own could not. However, just as the differences bring value to a relationship, they can also create conflict and problems as we share joint decisions and natural life preferences.

This is where an understanding of Typology can have value to the married couple or a close friendship. As we better understand one another and have a bit of a "handle" on why I and my spouse do things the way we do, we can begin to understand and accept those often irritating differences. The simple realization that we *are* different can be extremely valuable, and as we begin to gain a sense of peace about both my spouse's and my own goodness, with the grace of God we can even stop trying to change them.

The challenge is to begin to understand, to accept, and even to appreciate and *nurture* the differences that exist in our spouse and close friends. It seems that we spend much of our life finding someone who is interesting and complementary to our own personality, and then we set out on a lifelong quest to change them, even to make them an exact copy of ourselves! We need to communicate understanding, appreciation, and respect for the uniqueness of the other in our relationship. We can do this only by concentrating on the other's virtues. It can be helpful to study the sketch of our spouse or friend found in the Appendix. In this way we can get in better touch with their virtuous characteristics and begin to notice and even comment on them when they are evident. For example, if we learn in our spouse's sketch that he or she can be a very sensitive listener, we might comment on that trait when we see them using it.

We need to depend more on our spouse when a situation calls for application of their skills. For example, I (Bob) am a thinker and I make my decisions based on logic, facts, and justice. Carol Ann, on the other hand is a feeler, and her decisions take more circumstances and relationships into consideration. When we deal with correction and discipline of our children, we need both characteristics, so it is important for us to understand that we are coming from different perspectives. (I want to slug 'em, and she wants to hug 'em.)

As a result of using our type differences, we can more openly discuss the possibilities of how we will deal with a situation. Often we can take the best of both worlds and thus arrive at a more positive and useful course of action. As we will see in later chapters, there will come a time in our development toward wholeness when it will be necessary to cease depending upon our spouse to fill in for our weaknesses, and to grasp our undeveloped functions on our own.

At the same time, it can be helpful to look at the opposite characteristic of our *shared* preferences. For example, we are both strong intuitives. We both take in life in the form of whole ideas. We are future-oriented, and look at life's possibilities, or what "could be." When we look at the opposite of intuiting, we see the characteristics that are weak in our partnership, those of the sensing function, details, past experience, living in the present. It becomes helpful to see these traits as characteristics that do not come naturally for us but are important in certain situations.

Understanding the Tensions

Just as it can be helpful to understand the ways we can use our differences to live a fuller life, it is important to recognize the tensions that come about through the use of these differences. Below you will find some examples of tensions that might arise as a result of opposite types being married or in close relationships. Remember, too, that these tensions can come about between couples who share a preference but have significantly different strengths of it. For example, a couple might prefer judging, but one could have a much stronger preference for it than the other.

Introvert/Extravert Tensions

Some of the tensions that may exist for a couple consisting of an introvert and extravert may be in the area of sociability. The introvert may desire more space and time alone than the extraverted partner. The extravert may prefer a more active social life and the opportunity to interact with friends and relatives on a more regular schedule than the introvert. The extraverted partner may enjoy being with a larger group of people in new and untried situations, while the introvert will likely prefer a smaller group of well-known acquaintances.

In their communications, an introvert may prefer talking about their own and others' thoughts and feelings, while the extravert might desire talking of people, experience, and action-oriented topics. When they argue, the extravert will seem to have the upper edge as he or she "thinks on their feet" and has little hesitancy with conflict and confrontation. The introvert, on the other hand, will find the conflict draining and do their best thinking when they have a little time to process their thoughts. The introvert might have all the answers the next morning after they have thought about it overnight.

This need of the introvert to think things over can also have an effect on the shared decisions of the team. The extravert will tend to make quicker and sometimes more shallow decisions, while the introverted partner will take more time at it but the decisions are often better-thought-out.

Sensing-Intuiting Tensions

Some of the natural tensions between sensing and intuiting partners lie in the senser's preference for living in the "here and now," while the intuitive perspective is more future-oriented. (The intuitive mate will miss today's wedding anniversary but will have next summer's vacation well in hand!) The senser will be more concerned with the details while the mate will miss them but will have a better perspective on the whole picture.

This same perspective might be found in their arguments.

The senser will cite details, chapter and verse, that are very important to them, while the intuitive will be unimpressed and will want to talk more about the broader issues.

In financial planning, the senser is more apt to have detailed records of the income and the expenses, while the intuitive may not be interested in even looking at the figures. The latter is more interested in the final bank balance.

Thinking-Feeling Tensions

For a couple sharing opposite preferences on the thinking-feeling scale, tensions are apt to arise when they must share decisions. The thinker will be concerned with the logic and facts in the situation, while the feeler wants to consider more values and sentiment and relational harmony. The feeler wants to look at the circumstances and the people involved, while the thinking partner simply wants to decide based on truth and justice.

One of the most troublesome differences is the thinker and feeler's contrasting attitudes regarding discussion. The thinker sees *critique* as discussion, while the feeler is likely to take this form of "discussion" quite to heart. The thinker may have to say, "Gee, don't take it personally!" followed by "Why are you crying?"

This is all complicated by the thinker's likely preference to be brief and businesslike while the feeler will desire a more tender and personal approach to relationship.

Judging-Perceiving Tensions

The judging and perceiving tensions are likely to arise from the contrasting preferences of leaving options open and getting things decided. The judging partner will want to have things all decided and finished, while the perceiving mate will hesitate making final decisions and may even feel uneasy once they are made. The judger will want to plan their activities, be it for a weekend, vacation, or a lifetime, while the perceiver is just as apt to want to wait and see what happens.

When the perceiver makes a decision that disrupts the plans

of the judging partner, fireworks can erupt. The judger wants to know why the plans were changed, and the perceiver doesn't feel like the plans were all that important in the first place.

Love Is a Decision

Love is a decision. We know this term is worked over and over, but it has particular meaning and application when seen in the light of Typology. Our natural tendency is to behave in a particular way. This will be our spontaneous reaction, be it thinking, feeling, introversion, or whatever. But sometimes we have to put our natural preference aside in the name of love of our spouse or friend. We have to act outside of our normal comfort zone for their benefit. We have to avoid the temptation to do "what comes naturally." *This* is the decision to love. *This* is dying to one's self—one's natural self.

We cannot stand on the statement that "This is the way I am made." We each have some degree of freedom to choose our behavior. We are each responsible for the way we act. We can't use Flip Wilson's old line, "The devil made me do it." It is important that we each be willing to take responsibility and exercise this gift of Freedom.

This process begins with understanding. If we wish to take this tool seriously, we need to invest time in better understanding one another's personality. We need to know about our spouse or friend's type, talk about it, affirm them in the strengths mentioned in descriptions of their type, observe their type in action, become aware how we react to the qualities in them that are the opposite of our own, develop a respect for their characteristics, help them be all they were created to be.

Typology and Parenting

The main benefits that Typology brings to *all* relationships are acceptance and respect. This is true in our relationship with our children. If we are willing to understand Typology, we can begin to accept the fact that our children are made uniquely in

God's image and likeness and not in our own, and we might resist the temptation to try to make our children into copies of ourself.

Furthermore, we can begin to recognize that each of our children is not meant to be just like one another. Even identical twins may have vastly different personalities. If seen clearly, Typology can help us to see why *we* react differently to each of our children, why we treat them differently, and see that it is important that we do so. For example, our extraverted child may need ample opportunities to function in group situations such as team sports and scouting, while our introverted youngster may need encouragement in more solitary activities such as music lessons and reading.

As parents, our role is not only to respect differences, but even to *nurture* them. For example, in our own family of four, three of us are intuitives, and one, our daughter Sherri, is a senser. When I (Carol Ann) take a phone call for her, I think I have gotten about as much information as is necessary if I have the name and sex of the caller. However, for Sherri—our sensing, detail-oriented college student—that's not enough. A typical conversation might go like this:

> MOM: Sher, some girl named Sara called.
> SHERRI: What time did she call?
> MOM: I don't know, I think it was after dark.
> SHERRI: Was it before dinner or after? What did she say?
> MOM: I don't know. I think she's gonna call back.
> SHERRI: Oooh, Mom!

Sherri wants the details. Now I am trying to write them down, and I try to recall as many details as I can. She, on the other hand, is beginning to recognize that her intuitive mom and dad are utterly hopeless.

In using Typology in families, we are called not only to nurture the gifts and strengths of our children, but also to ever-so-gently try to encourage them to use and develop the skills of their opposite preferences. This latter task is much more difficult and some of the ideas suggested ahead in chapter 11 may be of assistance.

Typology is a tool that can be helpful. If you can use it in your family, rejoice. If you are the only family member interested, make the best use of it you can. We occasionally work with family groups where the children are older (sixteen or more), and the tool works well. If everyone takes an interest, it can have wonderful benefits. But the secret is to take it easy and have fun with it.

QUESTIONS FOR REFLECTION

1. Based on my understanding of the types, what is my type? What is my spouse or friend's type?

2. Based on our shared personality preferences—for example, both being introverts, both being thinking types, etc.—how do I see the strengths evident in our relationship?

3. After reading my spouse's or friend's sketch and reflecting, what are the differences in our personality types that cause the most tension? How?

4. In which characteristics of my spouse's or friend's type do I need to grow in acceptance and appreciation?

5. What characteristic in me causes the most tension with other family members?

9

The Value of Typology for Community

Before we address the value of Typology to those involved in communities, we think it is important to explain what we mean by community. We are speaking here of any group that works or lives together. The group could be a secular or a church work group, such as a place of business, a parish council, leaders of a prayer group, or a church staff. Community could also mean a religious community, or other groups which live together, such as a retreat center staff, or volunteer groups that share a community life.

Much of the value mentioned in the previous chapter dealing with couple and family relationships holds true in the community environment. This chapter can also be applied to family and marriage situations. As we've pointed out, Typology can be of significant help in the area of mutual understanding. Groups can grow significantly in their productivity, harmony, and Christian love if they realize that their individual differences can be extremely valuable, though not without tension. As in all relationships, be they family, marital, work, or communal, we need to respect the other people in our lives and begin to appreciate their unique characteristics.

Quite often, we find someone in our group whose words, actions, or attitudes seem to upset us. We find it difficult to put our finger on the exact cause and we wonder, "What is it that irritates us about so and so?" Perhaps it is something like a harshness we sense in them or the way they seem to pick at our ideas or opinions.

Frequently, the reason why someone irritates us is that we feel threatened by them. One of the reasons we can feel threatened by another's personality is that they are likely to be using one or more type characteristics that are the opposite of our own. For example, if we are a feeler, our own thinking function is not as well developed as is our feeling function. Thus, the "trust level" of our own thinking function is not very high. We may have had some poor experiences with this function when making decisions with logic, truth, and justice. Very likely this hasn't worked as well as our more trustworthy strength of using personal values, harmony, and relationship to make our decisions.

When we encounter a thinker using his or her well-developed strength, we don't always see *their strength* being used, but we see *our own poor experience and inadequacy* with that trait. This may cause an irritation in us, as we might *unconsciously* be thinking, "Considering how poorly the thinking function works for me, how could it be of value for them?" It is important to remember that their ability to use their personality strength (thinking) can be just as good or even better than our ability to use our own strength (feeling).

As was pointed out earlier, it is often these same opposite characteristics that draw us to certain people in the first place. Perhaps we can recall situations where we found an individual's personality very attractive to us when we first met them. However, after getting to know them better, we found some of those same personality characteristics to be very irritating.

Jung saw this as a "projection"—the unconscious transferring of some quality or characteristic of our own to some other person or object. When we are infatuated with a certain quality or qualities in someone, we are actually seeing what is hidden within ourselves. If we are an extraverted thinker, we might be attracted to a person who is a gentle and quiet introverted feeler. We are attracted to them because their behavior touches the hidden introverted feeling qualities within ourselves. This is projection, and nearly all relationships begin in this way.

As I (Carol Ann) look back at all of the close friendships in my life, I can clearly see that I have always been attracted to people who are the opposite of myself, especially on the introvert/extravert scale. I am a high introvert, and most of my close relationships have been with strong extraverts.

Another aspect I see is that most of my friends have been people who are strongly assertive. I find those traits attractive in others, and they also complement my own personality. To be truthful, I sometimes find that I clash with people of my own type. I often find them so much like myself that it is sometimes more difficult to get along.

While this may seem to be a somewhat positive aspect of projection, they are more often discovered not in an attraction to someone, but in a dislike for or irritation by someone such as the earlier example cited above. We can tell that we are projecting by the presence of an emotion that is out of proportion to the circumstances. If we find that we are very preoccupied by a habit of someone, or some fault, but, in reflecting, we see that there is no justification for our emotions to be so strongly engaged, we are likely to be in the grip of a projection.

We will speak more of projection in chapter 10, but for now it is helpful to understand that a projection ceases when we become aware that the unconscious characteristic we are projecting upon someone else is really a part of ourself. It is the *unconscious* which projects its contents upon others, and thus in this way shows them to us. When our ego becomes aware of the presence of these traits, they are no longer unconscious. The very process of acknowledging and embracing these hidden parts of ourself is the freeing process that allows us to look at someone else's behavior in an undistorted way. Over time, we can have *a more compassionate and truthful* view of the people in our family, group, or community as our unconscious reveals its contents. Here lies the wondrous benefit of the process of projection. It is through our projections that we learn of the content of our own unconscious. By looking at the qualities and characteristics of those to whom we are attracted and by whom we are significantly annoyed, we discover that wonderful and mysterious hidden self which we are endeavoring to reach and to make strong (Ephesians 3:16).

Projections can last for different lengths of time. Some go on for years, some for much shorter times. As we really get to know someone, we begin to see less and less of our own hidden characteristics and more and more of the true person upon whom we have been projecting. This is when the "honeymoon" is over and the irritations and *true love* begin. This is when our *true* personalities begin to interact with one another.

By looking at the people who irritate us in a group, we can learn much about ourselves. If we begin to work through our projections to lessen their effect upon us and upon the interaction of our group, we can do much to improve our group's effectiveness and our own self-knowledge.

Understanding Typology can also help us as we become aware of the contributions of the various functions in our group situation. We can know about the tensions that can surface between different types.

In their work *Please Understand Me,*[1] Dr. David Keirsey and the late Marilyn Bates highlighted the value that each personality type brings to those of the opposite type. It is these same contributions that each type brings to the group. Let us review them:

Sensers

In a group situation, sensers will be the ones to bring up the facts, apply past experience, and note what needs attention. They will ask the difficult questions and offer detailed suggestions or practical advice based upon what has happened in the past. Later in the implementation stages of an idea or project, the sensers will be the ones to have patience and encourage the group to do likewise. They will keep track of the details and be better equipped to face difficulties with realism.

Intuitives

As the future-oriented types, intuitives can be depended on by a group to bring up new possibilities and ideas. They will also supply creativity and ingenuity to the solution of difficult problems. They have the innate capacity to read signs of change, and thus they are able to help the group prepare for the future. It is also the intuitives who are likely to provide the enthusiasm a group needs and allow it to tackle difficulties. This comes about in part because the intuitives simply don't see all the details—and consequently the barriers—seen by their sensing counterparts.

Thinkers

The thinkers in the group will likely be willing to provide practical analysis to the group's situations. They will tend to find a plan's flaws in advance, and they will truly and objectively try to weigh the pros and cons of a set of decision alternatives. The thinkers will ultimately be the ones to organize a plan, and they will hold firm to policy when either internal or external forces challenge them or the group. Thinkers are also the ones better equipped to correct and discipline group members when it becomes necessary.

We see conflicts between thinking and feeling types as most prevalent in church leadership groups and communities. There seem to be two reasons for this. First is the high number of feeling types involved in church activities. It is not uncommon for our sessions with church groups to be attended by up to 80 percent feelers. Second, feelers have a tendency to judge thinkers as having "un-Christian" characteristics. The strengths of the thinker—logic, truth, and impersonal decisions—are simply not seen as valuable in church environments. Feelers look at thinkers and see them as cold, impersonal, critical, and rigid. Here again, if we find ourselves thinking this way, it's a good idea to look back at these thinking characteristics as seen in Jesus. These qualities are also made in God's image and likeness and can have significant value in all our groups.

Feelers

Finally, there is a real need for the qualities of the feeler in group situations. Because of their sensitivity to people, the feeler often provides the qualities needed to persuade others, conciliate factions when there is a problem, and forecast how others will feel about a proposal. Once a decision is made, the qualities of the feeler can arouse enthusiasm, sell and promote a project, and teach others about it. Feelers will add the element of appreciation to the entire team, as they are much more apt to provide affirmation to other members than are the thinkers.

Perceiving and Judging

The very nature of the difference between judging and perceiving makes them most vital to understanding a group's interaction. The judgers' preference is to make decisions, and the perceivers want to leave their options open and gather more information.

Because of this difference, judgers will look at the perceivers in their group and accuse them of being unable to make a decision, of being too loose and far too slow. Perceivers will see the judging types as "driving," too task-oriented, and too quick to jump to conclusions.

We once worked with a group of eight leaders. Seven of them were judging types, and one was a perceiver (he also happened to be the leader). When the group would discuss an issue, the seven judgers would leave their meeting confident that they had made a decision, while the perceiver would know they had not. As the group began to recognize their personality characteristics, they became better equipped to communicate and to be sure their decisions were *explicit*. They also became capable of laughing with one another when they saw those characteristics come into play in their interaction.

An effective group needs both perceiving and judging types to help slow them down or speed them up, as the case may require. Decisions do need to be made, but not too quickly, and not before the group has as much information as it needs.

Typology in Decision-making

One of the most significant contributions Typology can make to our groups is an increased awareness and appreciation of the different talents and gifts that are present. In reaching quality decisions, the challenge is to effectively utilize those many gifts. St. Paul speaks of this process:

"For as with the human body which is a unity although it has many parts—all the parts of the body, though many, still making up one single body—so it is with Christ . . . And indeed the body consists not of one member but of many . . . As it is, the parts are many but the body is one" (1 Corinthians 12:12, 14, 20).

A great deal of the time and energy spent by many groups is in reaching decisions and in carrying them out. Each group member comes to our group or community with a variety of personality strengths and weaknesses. If each of us truly values one another we can see that the area in which we are weak can be the area of strength for someone else. In our group decision-making we can come to a sense of dependency on one another and can know that corporately we will make a more viable decision than we would by ourselves.

This is part of the value of the tool of Typology. By using the experience, knowledge, and personality strengths of all the members of a group, a decision will be more broadly based and more thoroughly considered. As we have seen above, by calling for the gifts and talents of all the types—the feelers, thinkers, etc.—we can use the full range of information and personality processes we need to meet our mission.

However, as we all know, there is much more to the decision-making process than simply putting a group of different people together and expecting quality and well-thought-out decisions.

Our Decision-making Graph may be helpful to better understand what we mean. Looking at the vertical or up-and-down axis, we note the "differences in type" within a group. This ranges from a group with no type differences, at the bottom (a group of all one type, say INFP's or ENTJ's), to a group with all sixteen types represented, at the top.

Along the horizontal axis, the "quality" of the potential decisions ranges from a poor or "0" decision on the left to the absolutely "perfect" decision on the right. The more "alike" a group, that is, the less varied its types are, the less varied will

Decision-making Graph

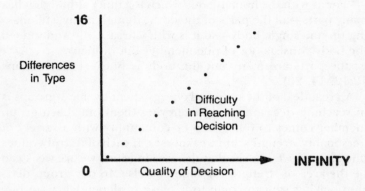

be the input that will go into its decisions. Thus, with limited data, it may not produce a decision with much "quality." That situation is represented on the lower left of the variable "Difficulty in Reaching Decision," as that low-quality decision will be relatively easy to reach. The group will tend to see everything from the same perspective and quite agreeably come to an easy and quick decision.

On the other hand, if the group is quite diverse, that is, with many different types represented, they are better able to reach a quality decision. They will take a full variety of facts into consideration and bring diverse styles of data-gathering and decision-making to bear upon the situation. Their decisions will, however, be more difficult to reach due to that very diversity.

"Z" Decision-making Model

However, by taking into consideration the various qualities of all the type functions, a group can use each function in an orderly manner regardless of the absence of persons preferring those functions.

This is known as the "Zigzag" or "Z" decision-making model. The basic concept is credited to Isabel Briggs Myers

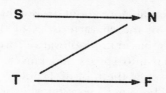

and is put into this graphic form by Dr. Gordon Lawrence in his book, *People Types and Tiger Stripes.* [2] The process presents an orderly flow of information-gathering and decision-making to be used in making individual or group decisions.

It begins by using the sensing function. That is, a group begins its decision-making process by first gathering all the relevant details and looking at everyone's experience concerning this situation. These details and experiences are recorded for the group to use. Next, the group uses its intuiting function and begins to "brainstorm." Members are invited to contribute all the possible decisions the group might reach. Nothing is considered too ridiculous. No one comments on the ideas. They are simply brought up and recorded in some way. This is the traditional "brainstorming" method.

Following these "perceiving" processes, that is, the gathering of data, the group calls its thinking function into play. Here, they apply all the logic and reason they can call forth to pass judgment on the previously offered possibilities. If something doesn't make sense, then the idea is ruled upon using the thinking gifts of facts, truth, justice, and logic. Finally, using the feeling function the group decides what is the *best* decision based on the circumstances. Here all the relationships, values, and what is best for the people involved come forward. This is not to say that the feeling function is the best decision-making function, but it is the best Christian approach *after* all the other functions have been used to analyze a situation. In this process, all of the strengths of the four functions are considered in an orderly fashion.

The tool of Typology can be a lot of fun if we understand it. It can be extremely interesting to watch those various dynamics in action and, with proper understanding, to discuss them, laugh, and make allowances.

Typology can reveal more about us. But, like any tool, it has its dangers. One of the characteristics of the tools used in scripture days was that in times of war or threat they could be heated and beaten into spears and knives. We must be on guard and never allow the tool of Typology to be used as a weapon. This tool becomes a weapon when we say such things as, "*This* is the way I am. I can't change. You must accept me." The decision to love we spoke of in the previous chapter on marriage has just as much application in community. We are called as Christians to be sensitive to those with whom God has called us to live and serve. Often we are unable to change those around us, but we are called to look at our *own* behavior in the light of the Gospel. (See 1 Corinthians 13.)

Along with the gifts that God has given us in our personalities is the capacity to lay those gifts aside in deference to the higher demands of love with regard to the needs of our brothers and sisters. He gives us the gift of *freedom* to make this choice when circumstances and the Gospel admonishment to love require. Let us try always to make use of this precious gift.

REFLECTION QUESTIONS

1. Who is the person with whom I am currently experiencing the most tension?

a. What are the strengths and virtues of this person?

b. How has this subject of Typology shed any light on the tensions in our relationship?

2. Based on this material, what are some of the likely strengths and weaknesses of my group (work, community, etc.)?

3. Which part of the material on decision-making is the most applicable to my group?

NOTES

1. David Keirsey and Marilyn Bates, *Please Understand Me* (Del Mar, Calif.: Prometheus Nemesis Books, 1984).

2. Gordon Lawrence, *People Types and Tiger Stripes* (Gainesville, Fla.: Center for Applications of Psychological Type, 1979), pages 57–65.

PART III

*Growth
and
Spirituality*

10

Understanding Development

One Step Further

When many are introduced to Typology, especially when they are in middle age or beyond, they can look back in their past and see that they used to behave in a more rigid and clearly defined way, but now they see themselves becoming more flexible. Perhaps they can see that their thinking function used to be their most dependable and frequently used form of behavior, but now they see themselves making more and more decisions taking into account more "feeling"-oriented characteristics.

While one doesn't normally change from one type to another, there is a valid reason to feel this way. This is often a signal that there is something going on in our growth and development process. There is progress being made, and it is reason for rejoicing. With God's grace, there is a call to grow and change as we move through life. While not all of us respond fully to this call, it is nonetheless there.

We have explained that one of each of the four pairs of characteristics make up our total type (either the extravert or introvert, sensing or intuiting, thinking or feeling, judging or perceiving). Introvert, extravert, judging, and perceiving are known as *attitudes,* and the balance are *functions.* Now we will focus more upon the *functions.*

Of our two *functions* (sensing or intuiting and thinking or feeling), each of us has a *dominant function*. Our dominant function will be one of the two functions found in our type. For example, if we are an ISFJ, our dominant function is sensing. (We'll show exactly how to determine your dominant function.)

This "dominant function" is likely to be our *most dependable,* our most well-developed personality characteristic. It is the one we use most frequently and upon which we rely most heavily. It was developed earliest in our life and we are most experienced in its use.

We have not only a dominant function, but also an auxiliary or second function, followed by a third and finally a fourth, or "inferior," function.

We grow and develop in our experience and confidence in using all four of these functions as we move through life. In explaining this growth we will draw upon the excellent work of Dr. W. Harold Grant, Sr. Magdala Thompson, R.S.M., and Fr. Thomas E. Clarke, S.J., whose hypothesis is elaborated in their book, *From Image to Likeness.* [1] Dr. Grant is the Director of the Missionary Cenacle Volunteers, Sr. Magdala is a Sister of Mercy currently in private practice in marriage and family therapy in Mobile, Alabama, and Father Clarke is a Jesuit priest, writer, and lecturer from New York. In addition to their book they have offered advance retreats and workshops using the theory of Typology.

According to the theory offered in their work, we develop each of our four functions at different ages. Also, we seem to develop them in a very definite order and progression. That is, first, our dominant function is developed, followed by the auxiliary, then the third, and finally the fourth. Before we go into the ages that this development seems to occur, understand that the ages are somewhat arbitrary and thus they are different for each of us. However, these ages might be considered the "norm" and thus they are quite useful in understanding the growth process. The ages are placed as follows:

0–6

From birth through age six, we seem to be relatively undifferentiated. That is, we use all of the functions somewhat spontaneously, but without really making any choices about how we will act. This might be seen by watching a four-year-old at play. At one moment, they can be very "sensing" as they play with a pile of little blocks and attempt to build a detailed building. At the next moment they have dropped the blocks and are daydreaming or sitting in your lap telling a wonderful fairy tale they have made up using their spontaneously unleashed intuiting.

6–12

From age six through about twelve, we begin to cultivate our dominant function. It is here that we become rooted in the behavior that we will depend upon most for the rest of our lives. This is when our personality begins to take its foundational form.

12–20

From twelve through twenty, we begin to develop our auxiliary function to provide an assistance to our dominant. During this time we begin to have an effective pair of characteristics. One of the functions will be a perceiving function, either sensing or intuiting, and the other will be a judging function, either thinking or feeling. That is, we will develop one trait to take in information using our sensing or intuiting plus we will develop a complementing dominant or auxiliary to act upon the world or make decisions, using either our thinking or feeling.

20–35

As we move into adulthood, from twenty to thirty-five, we begin to put our auxiliary function "on hold" a bit to work with our tertiary or third function. If we have developed our perceiving function of sensing or intuiting as our auxiliary during the previous period, we will now develop its opposite. Likewise, if the judging function of thinking or feeling was the work of the teen years, its opposite will come into play in the twenties.

35+

Finally, as we move into the second half of life, a little "time charge" seems to go off within us that demands that we work with our inferior function. This is often when the fun begins. This is when others (and ourselves) begin to wonder what is happening to us, and why we seem to be changing.

The authors of this theory hold that around the age of fifty we will become consciously "completed." That is, we will hopefully reach a point where we can begin to use all of our functions somewhat at will and return to our undifferentiated state of ages zero to six. However, this undifferentiated state is more *conscious* than our preschool period, in that we become more able to *choose* our behavior.

Before we get into a more detailed explanation of these, let us give you the tool to figure out which is your dominant, auxiliary, third, and fourth functions.

The chart below lists each of the sixteen types and next to them, in order, are the dominant, auxiliary, third, and fourth functions. The introverts are listed first, then the extraverts. Before you go on find your own type.

In the chart you will notice that your dominant and auxiliary functions are the two that are found in your type. (If you are an INFP, your dominant function is Feeling and your auxiliary is iNtuiting. The third function is the function that is directly opposite your auxiliary function (sensing), and the fourth is always the function opposite the dominant (thinking). Recall that each of the pairs are sets of *opposites*. Thus it stands to reason that our inferior or weakest function will be opposite of our strongest.

To fully understand this theory, we must first offer a deeper explanation of the two pairs of attitudes and their effect on how we use the four functions.

Introverts

Type	Dom	Auxl	3rd	Undev
	Intr	Extr	Intr	Extr
ISTJ	S	T	F	N
ISFJ	S	F	T	N
INFJ	N	F	T	S
INTJ	N	T	F	S
ISTP	T	S	N	F
ISFP	F	S	N	T
INFP	F	N	S	T
INTP	T	N	S	F

Extraverts

Type	Dom	Auxl	3rd	Undev
	Extr	Intr	Extr	Intr
ESFP	S	F	T	N
ESTP	S	T	F	N
ENFP	N	F	T	S
ENTP	N	T	F	S
ESTJ	T	S	N	F
ESFJ	F	S	N	T
ENFJ	F	N	S	T
ENTJ	T	N	S	F

The Introvert/Extravert Attitudes

There is a significant difference in the ways in which the introvert and the extravert live their lives. You will recall that the extravert is a person who prefers to live in the outer world. They are said to be a very "up front" people. As they live out in the world with the rest of us, their personality is relatively easy to see. They tend to show us and the rest of the world all of their strengths and abilities. If an extravert is a dominant thinker, he or she uses that thinking function in their extraverted attitude, that is, in their dealings with the world. Likewise, the extravert uses their secondary function, or auxiliary, more in their inner world, in their quiet time, in their private, inward thoughts.

An introvert is one who prefers the inner world of ideas and feelings, dealing with things interiorly, the quiet, the inside. Thus, an introvert who has a dominant thinking function will use this strength in their more significant and private *inner world*. It is their auxiliary or second function which they use for their dealings with the outer world. It is that auxiliary characteristic that we, the world, tend to see because that is the function they choose to use for dealing with us. Their strength or dominant function is reserved for their more comfortable inner world.

The Judging/Perceiving Attitudes

We mentioned when we described the attitudes of judging and perceiving that these attitudes were never explicated by Jung. While they were implied by his work, their identification came about more as a result of the observations of the developers of the Myers-Briggs Type Indicator. Further, we noted that the judging attitude, because it was the "decision-making" attitude, was a "generic function" directly linked with the "specific functions" of thinking and feeling. Sensing and intuiting are the "specific" functions associated with the "generic" perceiving function.

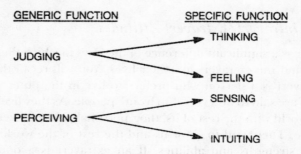

The MBTI is a measurement of personality preference as seen *by the world*. When we answered the questions, or guessed our type, we did so pertaining to how we treat the outside world, not our more private inner world. Thus, if we scored as a judging, this tells us we prefer to use our judging function with the *outside world,* regardless if we are an introvert or extravert.

Let's look at an example. For Bob, an ENTJ, his extraverted attitude tells us he is going to use his dominant function out front with the world. With an extravert, "what you see, is what you get." In addition, because he scored as preferring the "judging" attitude, we can see that his dominant function will be his *judging* function, or thinking or feeling, whichever he scored. For Bob, that judging function is his thinking. That is our first step in better understanding Bob's personality. The dominant function for an ENTJ type is thinking. The auxiliary function is always the other function of the type—in this case, intuiting. This again makes infinite sense, as we are meant to have a pair of complementing functions, one perceiving (S/N) and one judging (F/T).

The third or "tertiary" function always is opposite of the auxiliary, or, for Bob, sensing, and, finally, the inferior function is always the opposite of the dominant—feeling, in Bob's ENTJ case.

As a recap, for an extravert the ability to understand their type is direct. When we look at the judging/perceiving attitude, this preference will send us directly to the *dominant function.* If the generic function is judging, the dominant specific function will be the preferred thinking or feeling. If the generic function is perceiving, the dominant specific function will be the preferred sensing or intuiting of the type. The auxiliary will be the "other" preferred function of the type, the third will be opposite of the auxiliary and the inferior will be opposite of the dominant.

Let's look at the introvert. They are only a bit more complicated. When we look at an introvert's type, we can use the same method as for the extravert, but we have to remember that this will lead us to the function the introvert uses to deal with the *outside world.* As it is the *inside world* that is most comfortable for an introvert, this function will be their auxiliary. They reserve the use of their dominant function for their preferred interior world. Thus we have to look further to identify it.

Let's use Carol Ann's type, INFJ. Her introversion signals us

that we must look a step further than for an extravert to find
her dominant. When we look at her generic judging and perceiving, her preference for judging points us to her preferred
thinking/feeling function, or, for her, feeling. This is the function that Carol Ann will use most in her dealings with the
outside world. But because she is an introvert, and type measures her dealings with the outside world, we learn this is her
auxiliary or second-best function that she uses in the outer
world. Her dominant function, the function she reserves for
use in her preferred inner world, is her perceiving function, or
intuiting. As with the extravert, the third function is opposite
of the auxiliary, or thinking, and the inferior is opposite of the
dominant, or sensing.

On the chart on page 83 you will find one row of information
not yet mentioned. At the head of each column you will see
alternating "Intr/Extr" notes. These denote how the function
is used. For example, in the extrovert chart, we see that they all
use their dominant function in their preferred outside world.
Thus, the dominant function column is noted as "Extr," or
extraverted. Likewise, as mentioned, they use their auxiliary
function for the inner world, and that column is noted "Intr,"
or introverted. The theory says that as we grow and develop
our third and fourth functions, we will alternate between introverted use and extraverted use. The chart notes the progression of the theory.

Introducing the Inferior Function

The inferior function is the one we are least likely to call upon
and is our least dependable characteristic. It is the extreme
opposite of our strong right or left hand. However, unlike our
right and left hands, we cannot use our dominant and inferior
functions at the same time. We cannot be taking in information
through the sensing and intuiting functions simultaneously.
Information comes either in details or in whole possibilities.
Likewise, we cannot make decisions with both our thinking
(using logic) and feeling (using relationships and personal
values) at the same time. We must put one "on hold" to use the
other.

It's important to remember that just because this inferior function is our least developed, it doesn't mean that we will never use it. Indeed we do. As a matter of fact, this least developed function demands that we use it almost as if it had a spirit of its own. It is part of our being, but it is rooted deep in our unconscious. Our problem is that we often don't have much practice with its use. We are much more comfortable using its opposite, which is our dominant and strongest trait.

When this inferior function is required to be used, we are not likely to deal with it very well, and we may act a little erratic when we use it. This is a vital part of this characteristic and we will talk about it in some detail in the next chapter.

Before we go on, let us offer a dissenting opinion on the ages of the development hypotheses mentioned above. Our own experience, and that of many others, indicates a much less ordered development than this theory suggests. There could be many reasons for this, and we will discuss a number of them. However, an alternative theory suggests simply that during the first half of life, that is, prior to mid-life (mid-life occurs somewhere between thirty-five and sixty), we develop our dominant and auxiliary functions, and during the second half of life (after mid-life), we develop our third and fourth or inferior functions. There is much in Jung's basic concepts that supports this configuration.

We are comfortable with either theory, but we will proceed with the concept suggested by *From Image to Likeness* as it lends itself to a fuller explanation of the developmental process.

Our experience is that when we begin to speak about "growth and development," this is where Christians want to jump right into being "whole and complete." For some reason, we want to have all of our development work behind us. We seem to shy away from the idea that there is plenty of work ahead of us, especially if we are judging types. Our own observation and experience plus that of many other practitioners share the view that while this development process certainly describes the goal, it rarely if ever seems to be reached. It is not important if we are "on target" age-wise, that we are developing the function called for in the theory. It is more important that we are mindful of the process and are open to nurturing the changes as they are called forth within us. This development process is the goal of the lifelong journey, and even though we desire to reach our destination of wholeness, we will do so only in the presence of the Lord.

The goal, then, is to become *more free* as opposed to becoming *finally free.* Let's not allow someone to convince us we have no more work to do because we have hit our fifty-first birthday, or any other milestone. God gives us the rest of our lives to work on this journey and that is why most of us over thirty-five need to continue to work on our undeveloped and inferior functions.

Development Can Be Suppressed

A significant understanding is helpful at this point. Our growth and development can be suppressed at different stages of our life for a host of reasons. Our environment, be it family, work, school, or our culture in general, may be such that it has not supported the development of our "scheduled" functions. Suppose I am unconsciously trying to develop my auxiliary feeling function during the period from age twelve to twenty. During this time, I will want to be growing in my decision-making, using personal values, harmony, and relationships. If I happen to live in a family that is thinking-oriented, they may well stifle that growth by sending signals that my decisions based on such values are "soft" and "sissy" and not what "big boys" do. This causes a situation known as *falsification of type.*

This might happen to a developing intuitive who is growing up in a sensing environment. Often their lack of concern for details and past experience might be seen as weakness and the family or school might be telling the youngster in many ways that he or she had better "shape up" if they are going to get anywhere. It is a generally accepted fact in Typology that traditional primary school situations support the talents of the detail-oriented senser more than the free-thinking intuitive.

These are only examples, as our environment may support or reject any of the functions depending on the preferences of those around us.

If we have had these "negative signals" sent to us about our preferred behavior, later in life we will have to walk through the process of embracing and developing these suppressed functions before we can move on effectively to the development of our third and fourth functions.

This is where we might use the process known as healing of memories. We can spend time going back to those times in our lives when we were unable to behave as we naturally preferred. We can recall times when we were criticized for behavior that seemed natural and right and ask the Lord to heal those memories and give us the strength to move on in our growth.

Cultural Bias

We mentioned earlier that culture can also have an effect on our freedom to choose. For example, 60 to 65 percent of our culture is comprised of extraverts. There is often a tendency to see introverts as "unusual" or "strange." Something must be wrong with them (or us), as they tend to be so quiet and like to be alone.

For those who grew up in the sixties or before, our Western culture seemed to support certain unique characteristics in its men and women. It is said that the type bias, the type our Western culture has promoted in the past for its men, is for extraversion, sensing, thinking, and judging, or ESTJ. For women, it is said to be for introversion, intuiting, feeling, and perceiving, or INFP. While our women of the eighties may object to this bias, it is perhaps more clear when answering the question "What type characteristics has our culture instilled in our young girls in the past?" The male bias seems much more obvious and stronger than for the female bias, but it is important to recognize if and how our own preferences are opposed to this bias. If we are a man other than an ESTJ, or a woman other than an INFP, we may have not been supported in our early development and may need to do some "homework" before we can successfully hurdle the developmental tasks of our later years. This cultural bias seems to be changing now as the whole issue of women's rights and equal opportunity begins to take root in the American culture.

Goal—Freedom

The goal of this journey is *freedom*—freedom to choose our behavior. All four of these functions are *good*. We need all of them. But our natural tendency is to choose one more than the other. As we move through life, God calls us to fully embrace and use all of these characteristics. This is the goal of this developmental journey: to be able to use thinking, feeling, sensing, intuiting, and all of the attitudes for which our circumstances in life call and as the Gospel dictates. We don't want to be driven by spontaneous behavior. We want to have all the tools of human behavior at our disposal *and* to have the freedom to use them.

Freedom is a process that needs to unfold. It is difficult to put age limits and standards on our journey to freedom and God. All of us desire freedom, yet we must be honest in accepting where we are on our journey. If this means that we are sixty years old and find that we should be working on our auxiliary or third function, we must be willing to accept this reality. There is no sin or condemnation in our journey. The only risk is in not being honest with ourselves.

Likewise, if we are twenty-five, and decide that we are so free that we must get down to the business of developing our *inferior* function, one must wonder if we are being honest and patient with ourselves. Before we can reach the goal, we must allow ourselves all the growth opportunities and time that we need.

Freedom isn't a race, but a slow and gradually unfolding process that usually takes a lifetime. We are truly free only when we meet Jesus face to face. So relax. Be accepting of wherever you may be on your journey, ever asking the Lord for the grace to move forward and the desire to change and grow.

Strength of Preferences

We promised in the last chapter that we would return to the issue of MBTI "scores." If we are going to develop our undeveloped functions, that is, our third and fourth functions, it is vital that we have a firm appreciation of our dominant and auxiliary functions. We must also develop skill in their use. This means that we need a confidence in *who we are*, in how God has made us. Without this confidence, we are unlikely to have the freedom to move on to our third or fourth function. If, for some reason, we are consciously or unconsciously rejecting the characteristics with which we have been endowed, we are not going to have the freedom to move on and embrace their opposites.

Using any function involves a freedom to let go of its opposite function. If, for example, I have a confidence and comfort that I am a sensing/feeling person, and I appreciate that these qualities are good and made in God's image and likeness, then, and only then, will I have the freedom to set these strengths aside and embrace the opposite intuiting/thinking behavior. Otherwise, when the time comes to use these undeveloped traits, I will see the necessary behavior as threatening, or I won't have the necessary confidence in my identity to put my dominant or auxiliary aside to nurture this opposite. This freedom also requires that I have an appreciation and respect for these opposite qualities in order to see them as valuable.

This is usually a very difficult process for all of us: to let go of that which is developed, to let go of those traits with which we are most skilled and comfortable. Yet, at the same time, if we truly see and accept the giftedness of our personality and pray for the inner healing that is needed, we will, with God's grace and help, move on to change and grow.

This is where the MBTI scores can be of help. If the score (not the points) for either the dominant or auxiliary function is a "low" score (9 or less), this *might* be an indication that our confidence and acceptance level of this characteristic is low and we need to do some developmental "homework." A low score might also mean that we have a balanced preference between this characteristic and its opposite. (The former is the more usual case than the latter.)

We say *"might"* because the MBTI measures only one of the three elements we believe go into the use of a function. First (the element measured by MBTI) is our preference to use a particular function. The scores indicate the strength of that preference. In other words, how strong is my desire to use this function over its opposite? For example, if I am a feeler, the score of the MBTI will give an indication of how much stronger my desire is to make decisions using harmony, relationships, and personal values over the thinking counterpart process using logic, impersonal values, and justice.

The second element that determines our use of a function, and one not measured by the MBTI, deals with *skill level.* That is, do I have the practice and basic skills to use this function? For example, what is my capacity to apply logic and facts to make a decision using the thinking function? Skill level comes from practice in using a function. A thinking person, whose life has been spent in a thinking family and whose career utilizes only thinking decisions, might rarely have been in circumstances that have given them an opportunity to use the feeling function and thus they may have developed very little skill in its use.

The final element in the use of a function, and again, not measured by the MBTI, is *freedom.* I need to ask myself, "Do I have the unconscious and conscious *freedom* to choose this behavior when appropriate?" My level of freedom can go back to my experience of using the function. If, for example, every time I've tried to anticipate the future and consider the "possibilities" using my intuitive function I have been laughed at and ridiculed, my freedom may be restricted. I may have unconsciously put aside that function and fear using it. This may also come about from using my stronger or dominant functions to pass judgment on the use of its opposite. Perhaps I may use my dominant feeling function to assess the "success" of a decision I made using my inferior thinking function's truth, justice, and logic. I may conclude, because some people were hurt in the process of the decision (even justifiably so), that this function has no value and, as a result, I may unconsciously put it aside.

Each of these elements—preference, skill, and freedom—can be enhanced by prayer, patience, practice, and decisions. We can only increase our skill levels in using a trait by practicing them, by consciously bringing those latent skills into use. As we will highlight in the next chapter, we don't do so during times when we are under pressure. If we are weak in making "feeling" decisions, we don't go to work tomorrow morning and decide to use our feeling function all day. We need to be gentle with ourselves. Gentle and prayerful.

We invite you to look at these elements in your own development process. Reach back and reflect upon your own history, your skill level, preference strength, and your freedom. It is important that the information in this chapter and the next be applied and worked through in the experience of our lives. It is not enough simply to "know about" this information. The reflection question at the end of this chapter could be the turning point of making this topic one that will be a breakthrough in your life.

REFLECTION QUESTIONS

1. (Use chapters 2–5 as a reference.) Based on your ability to use the characteristics of your dominant and auxiliary functions, does it appear that you are ready to develop your third or fourth function, or do you need to go back?

2. According to the theory, from age six to twelve we develop our dominant, and from age twelve to twenty we develop our auxiliary. Did your family situation in those years support or suppress development of your dominant and auxiliary?

3. Based on your type and the cultural bias for your sex (ESTJ for men and INFP for women), what need do you see for development work?

4. If you have children, reflect on where they are in their development, based on your guess of their type. What pattern can you see in their present stage?

NOTES

1. W. Harold Grant, Magdala Thompson, Thomas E. Clarke, *From Image to Likeness* (New York: Paulist Press, 1983).

11

Development of the Inferior Function

"Then, speaking to all, [Jesus] said, 'If anyone wants to be a follower of mine, let him renounce himself and take up his cross every day and follow me. Anyone who wants to save his life will lose it; but anyone who loses his life for my sake, will save it' " (Luke 9:23–24).

To be a follower of Jesus we need to renounce ourself and this means to let go of our strengths. We must put aside our stronger and more confidently used functions and take up our cross and embrace our weaknesses. Our weaknesses are our undeveloped or inferior functions.

The holiness and freedom we seek can only be found by letting go of our strengths to embrace our weaknesses.

Before we go further into this subject of understanding our inferior functions, let us first speak of Jung's concept of the "shadow." The shadow consists of parts of our personality which we have, for one reason or another, repressed into our unconscious. These parts are characteristics within us that our ego denies as existing. The shadow usually manifests itself as an inferior trait for which there has been an unconscious decision that it is not wanted as a part of oneself and consequently we deny its very existence.

For example, we may have an unconscious tendency to hoard our possessions. This is a characteristic we dislike and have rejected as a part of ourselves. However, the tendency is real and forms a part of a hidden personality within us that has a great influence on our behavior.

We may also have a positive shadow which appears when we tend to identify more with our negative qualities and repress the positive ones. We may feel particularly drawn to someone who is gentle and kind but cannot see those qualities in our own personality because they are repressed.

The shadow, which seems to have an energy of its own, makes itself known primarily through a process we spoke of earlier known as *projection*. Projection takes place when we literally "project" a repressed shadow characteristic onto another person or circumstance. For example, one whose shadow side has that selfish, hoarding characteristic mentioned above might be totally enraged when they see someone saving string or behaving in a similarly innocent frugal manner. When this happens, we are said to have been "hooked" by the other person and have projected our own hidden and disdained characteristic upon them.

This also happens with positive characteristics. We might find ourselves hopelessly infatuated by someone whose behavior "hooks" our own hidden positive, yet repressed characteristics. Again, using the example cited earlier, we might be bewildered to find ourselves uncharacteristically drawn to someone whose warmth and gentleness "taps into" our own similar characteristics. As a matter of fact, all romantic love begins with projections of our positive shadow side.

One of the key ways to identify the existence of a projection is to see that our emotions are out of proportion to a situation. If I find myself with a more highly charged emotional response than the situation warrants, there is a good possibility that a projection is at work. These projections are a tool the Lord gives us to help us see our shadow side. The process of coming to freedom is greatly aided by becoming aware of our projections. It is helpful to find those characteristics within ourself and begin to acknowledge and even "befriend" them. In so doing, these parts of our "hidden self" which we have mentioned frequently lose more and more of their unconscious control over us. We can become increasingly free of these seemingly irrational outbreaks of highly emotional projections when we are willing to acknowledge them and work with them.

We can make great strides in bringing our shadow side into the light of our consciousness by using the tool of Typology. While our undeveloped functions do not comprise all of the material of our shadow, these functions will "flavor" all of the rest of the shadow. Remember that all four functions, sensing, intuiting, thinking, and feeling, reside within each of us. To the extent that we deny these characteristics within ourself they will reside in our shadow and reveal themselves through projections. Thus, as we continue on this subject of developing our inferior functions, we can speak in terms of "befriending our shadow."

The Spirituality of Typology

The most spiritual aspect of the subject of Typology is found in understanding the journey to which each of us is called in developing and accepting our opposite type. We are all called to freedom: to develop and use all four of our functions. On this journey, we have found the most difficult task is in developing the inferior function. This is because it involves a real dying to ourself and sometimes a painful process of putting our strengths, our identity, on "hold" in order to develop our opposite or inferior function. We need to embrace and befriend what is naturally uncomfortable to us and integrate it into our lives.

As always, Jesus shows us the way. We find our model in Jesus's life and the way he used all of the functions freely. One function did not dominate the others. Although we will never reach the level of absolute freedom that Jesus experienced, he is our model as we grow in our freedom to choose the function that can best deal with the situation at hand.

This freedom to choose, that we speak of in Jesus, was also a developing process for him. The Gospels tell us mostly of the last three years of his life, but the thirty years before were a time of growth for him, just as in our own lives. In his humanity, in his experiencing all of the human condition, he too had to grow and to adapt. At the end of the second chapter of

Luke, following Jesus's stay in Jerusalem after the Passover feast, we are told that he "increased in wisdom, in stature, and in favor with God and with people."

We can also find our model of freedom in the Incarnation itself. Our God is infinite. He has no bounds, no beginning, no end. Before the Incarnation, Jesus was so certain of his identity, so certain of being "infinite," so confident that he was from God the Father, that he was able to put his "infinity" aside and embrace or *become* his opposite. The opposite of being infinite is to become "finite," to become human, with all the limitations that humanity entails. In the Incarnation, God accepted his opposite. To have the freedom to do so, he had to be so rooted and confident in who he was that he did not feel vulnerable in accepting that opposite.

Here too is our journey: to be so rooted in our identity—the way God made us—that we can be free enough to put aside the behavior we naturally prefer and embrace behavior which does not come naturally—our opposite.

Here rests the theology and the spirituality of our journey: a journey to the freedom of which we have been speaking throughout this book, a journey clearly pioneered by the Father in the act of creation, a journey clearly walked by the Son in the Incarnation, a journey to which each of us is called in order to become all that God intends for us.

We believe we can grow on this journey by using the tool of Typology. We can become more rooted in who we are by accepting, practicing, and developing those strengths God has given us. At the same time, we need to be aware of the journey to accept, practice, and develop the inferior side, our weaknesses.

We will now look at how we know when that inferior side is surfacing, demanding attention, often through our projections. We will look at how to deal with it and how to develop it into becoming a strength for us.

Surfacing of the Inferior

In the previous chapter, we spoke of the need to develop the inferior functions during the second part of our life, but let us remember that to *survive*, we have all used our inferior functions all through life. It is during this second half of life that we are called to develop and own this part of ourself.

Our inferior functions will seem to demand attention from us in rather unusual ways. Often, they will surface when we are weakened—perhaps fatigued, depressed, under pressure—or during an argument. For example, a dominant sensing type may be subject to negative intuitions such as anxieties and fears about the future and the possibilities it holds. A dominant thinker's inferior feeling function may cause them to become overwhelmed by negative, unrecognized moods. A dominant feeler may find themselves "taken over" by a tremendous sense of rigid "logic" as their thinking function comes to the surface. Finally, a dominant intuitive may discover that they have been "overwhelmed" by a string of "sensing" details about the past that normally hold no interest for them.

Characteristics of the Inferior Functions

The inferior functions build up a connection between the conscious and the unconscious. As a result, they can be our key to becoming an integrated, free person, a person who can access the latent possibilities of the bountiful unconscious.

As we can see by the next drawing,[1] the inferior function is the function most rooted in the unconscious. When material from either the collective or the personal unconscious needs to surface, the path of least resistance will be the inferior function. It is for this reason that we say the shadow takes on the "flavor" of the inferior function.

In the book *Jung's Typology,*[2] Marie-Louise von Franz writes of the inferior functions in much detail. The first part of the book comes from her lectures at the C. G. Jung Institute in Zürich, Switzerland. Her work is extremely helpful for those who desire a deeper understanding of the inferior functions.

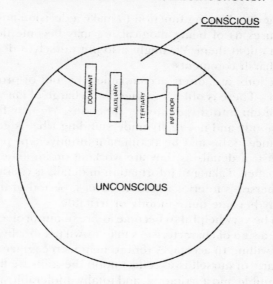

**DEPTHS OF THE FUNCTIONS
IN THE UNCONSCIOUS**

How to Recognize the Inferior Functions

When the inferior functions come to the surface, we are said to feel very foolish or very bold. We can feel elated about ourself or be in a state of despondency and gloom. We seem to be at one extreme or the other. When we are using the inferior functions in a conscious way, their use is generally slow compared to our use of our dominant or auxiliary functions. They are simply not used as competently and are slower and usually more awkward—much like trying to use our opposite hand to write our name.

We can experience a sensitivity when someone is critical of our work or behavior which involves these functions. We may become extremely defensive. This is often because our opinion about our ability to use these functions satisfactorily is not very positive. We believe ourself to be inadequate in this weakest area, so we can be easily influenced by another's similar judgments. For example, if we are a dominant feeler and we

are using our thinking function to make a decision and someone accuses us of being illogical, we may become defensive
and lash out at them. We might also put ourselves down with
unduly harsh comments.

Projections are often accompanied by out-of-proportion
emotions. There is often a tremendous charge of emotion felt
when we tap into these inferior functions. We may find ourselves moody and not really understanding what is going on.
An instance of this may be a dominant intuitive type providing
a long list of details as they are working on an extensive research paper. Taking in information in details is characteristic
of this person's inferior function. After a period of time, this
type may become quite moody or irritable.

It can be very helpful to become aware of our projections, as
they are a sign of characteristics in our own personality that we
are not willing to accept. A tool to help us recognize some of
these parts of ourself is to reflect upon the traits we find most
contemptible, most irritating, and totally intolerable in others.
These same traits may be the personality traits of our undeveloped or inferior functions.

Dealing with the Inferior Functions

The main thing to remember in dealing with inferior functions
is to give ourself time. We must be patient and not expect to
use the inferior functions with the same proficiency as we use
our dominant functions.

It is best to deal with these inferior functions with humor,
realizing that it takes time to develop them and that there is
tremendous gain to be made from the effort.

Using our inferior function requires a constant attention to
it while it is in use. A good visual aid is to imagine yourself
keeping your thumb on the button while using it. For example,
if you are trying to develop the feeling function, you will need
to "keep your thumb on the feeling button" while trying to use
that function. Sometimes it will "slip off" and you will revert
back to your natural thinking function, but when you become
aware of it, put your thumb back on it.

It is important, if possible, to avoid involvement in activities that require a high use of these functions when we are physically tired or under stress. There should be times when we can consciously put aside our dominant or auxiliary function and allow our third or inferior functions the time and space they need to develop. For this reason, the inferior is better left to times of "optional behavior," that is, times when we can more easily choose to bring them into use. Such times often involve our use of leisure, times when we *choose* our activities. Another key opportunity is our prayer time. For this reason, we will devote the next chapter to prayer.

The "bottom line" is to try to be balanced. We need to call the traits into action, but at the same time we must try to be neither super-critical nor self-pitying if they don't work so well. Remember, this is a lifelong journey and we have plenty of time. We must be patient with ourself.

The Role of Grace

Growth does not come by our own efforts alone. We grow with God's grace. Only he can give us the desire, the power, and the patience to move forward on this journey. Thus, as we look at these ideas, we should ask God to guide us and give us all the grace we need to become the unique "child of God" that he desires.

Suggestions for Growth

What follows are some suggestions that can be used if we are trying to develop one or more of the functions. These suggestions are designed primarily to develop our inferior functions, but they can also be used if we are doing some "homework," that is, if we are trying to go back and strengthen our dominant or auxiliary or third functions.

A general technique that can have benefit is to pray about the parts of ourselves we dislike. Journaling our thoughts and feelings in this area may be helpful. Sometimes this objectivity allows us to become more conscious of the functions and their use.

As a feeling type, an example for me (Carol Ann) might be in handling a problem with one of our children, knowing that I must make a decision using logic and justice. I can know this in my mind, but find it difficult to execute. By focusing upon the frustration I experience and writing how I feel and what goes on inside of me when something like this happens, I may begin to grow in understanding the root of my frustration. I may be able to see what is truly behind it and begin to deal with it in my life. An excellent book for further reading on this topic is *Keeping Your Personal Journal* by George Simons.

Developing the Sensing

The dominant intuitive is the one who sees the possibilities in situations and likes solving new problems. They are usually impatient with routine details. They are always looking around the corner. Thus, to develop our inferior sensing function, we need to consciously slow down our pace of life. We need to stop and listen to the sounds around us for a period of time, even if it's for only thirty seconds. Listen to the silence, or look around you and become *really aware*. It is said that once we are able to look at a tree or a star and see a miracle, then at last we have truly seen.

Become aware of how little we really enjoy our leisure, as this is another weakness of the dominant intuitive. This may reflect our unwillingness to enjoy the "present moment." Perhaps we need to develop some sensing hobbies that call for much attention to detail. For instance, working with clay, woodworking, drawing, astronomy, or building a detailed model by following the instructions. Remember, be patient with yourself.

Recently we were on an extended retreat, and during each day we had about two hours of free time. I (Bob) decided to work on the development of my tertiary sensing function. Every day I went out and, with great care and attention to detail, waxed our car. I had not waxed one of my cars since I was eighteen, and paying attention to all of that detail *did not come naturally*. But it was a good experience.

To develop our sensing, we could take a walk in the woods and try to be attentive to color, form, motion, birds, trees, animals, insects, or leaves. An exercise we have tried is to take a pencil and paper into the woods and sit down in front of a tree and write down every detail we can see about the color, size, shape, texture, using all of our senses.

Developing the Intuitive

The dominant sensing type gathers information in detail and uses the five senses. They like to live in the present moment rather than the future. In order to develop the intuitive function, we may need to be wary of excessive neatness in our personal and relational lives. We might start with something simple, like leaving the bed unmade one morning.

Perhaps through the use of our journal, we might look at our hopes and dreams for the future, as the dominant senser dislikes looking far ahead. We might choose a symbol from nature that expresses some aspect of our life as it is now, or as it has been, or as we would like it to be. A symbol always stands for something more than its obvious or immediate meaning.

An example for me (Carol Ann) is the daisy. The daisy is an aspect of myself, a symbol of simplicity and who I am. It is a symbol of the way I would like to live my life. It is a plant which grows in the fields or along the road and is often not confined to a flower garden. To me, the daisy symbolizes the freedom I desire in my life, the freedom to live to my full potential, being led by the Spirit. I see in the daisy a delicacy and a simplicity I desire in my personhood, in my relationship with God, and in my surroundings.

In developing our intuiting function, we need to see that there is truly no end to the possibilities of our personality. We need to be able to look at the details of our personality and see how they manifest themselves and realize that there is much more. We have much more potential than we can see at the present moment. What we may view as limitations of our personality may truly be transformed into gifts and potential for growth. If, for example, our dominant and auxiliary are thinking and sensing, respectively, we need to recognize that our more limited feeling and intuiting lie deeper in our unconscious. They may be more difficult to deal with and integrate into our personality, but the potential for growth is there. It is in seeing this very reality that we develop our intuiting function.

In developing our intuiting, we need to expect the best from others. We need to *look beyond the details* to the *potential* in the person. This is especially true for that "special" person who seems to bother us the most.

Developing Thinking

If we are a dominant feeling person we are likely to make decisions with a concern for harmony and with a concern about our own or another's personal likes or wishes. To put those preferences aside and develop our thinking function we need to make our decisions using logic, order, and impersonal analysis.

To do so, we might try to foster a sense of order and regularity in our prayer lives. The sacrament of reconciliation or visits to our spiritual director may help foster this sense of structure.

Try to develop assertiveness. (This is especially true for *introverted* feelers trying to develop thinking.) We need to try to express what we want to do and say in a way which respects our own dignity and that of others. Practice saying "no" without belittling ourselves or making excuses or feeling guilty.

Make a conscious effort to cultivate both oral and written communications skills. Put to use objective thought and attempt to formulate clear verbal communications.

I (Carol Ann) have had much experience of this during the past few years. For Bob, an extraverted thinker, public speaking comes naturally. But, as an introverted feeler, I find speaking before a group very difficult, at least until I've started. I also find that I'm constantly writing and rewriting my talks in an attempt to clarify and communicate more clearly. (This book might never have been finished were it left to me.) Thus, communication is an area in which I have to work and it does not come naturally. Yet, I have found myself to be a very effective speaker and it proves very energizing and rewarding as part of my journey to God.

A feeler trying to develop their thinking might cultivate a

relationship with a dominant thinker. In this relationship, the feeler might be able to express opinions and criticisms without the other person taking it "personally," as another feeler might.

We may also invest ourself in justice ministries. While a dominant feeler may have been involved in mostly compassionate ministries serving the needs of others, they may need to change to more *administrative or organizational* roles, such as raising funds for the poor or organizing a "Right to Life" march.

Finally, one developing the thinking function might create a chart of how they presently use their time compared with how it could be used more efficiently. This is especially helpful if combined with a list of priorities.

Developing Feeling

A person whose dominant function is thinking will be one who is logical and concerned with truth and justice. They may appear to be unconcerned or unaware of what is happening on an interpersonal basis. Therefore they will need to develop their feeling function. To do so they might cultivate intimacy with God and with other people. They might be attentive to tenderness and affection toward others. Perhaps a married thinker trying to develop his/her feeling might plan a romantic evening out with their spouse.

We will need to consciously strive to complement others, as this can be extremely difficult for dominant thinkers.

In the journey of developing inferior feeling, it might be helpful to remember special moments of intimacy in our past: family traditions, emotional times, perhaps marriage, the birth of a child, ordination, or solemn vows.

Developing the feeling function can also be aided by developing the skill of *empathy*. We can try to place ourself in the shoes of another. Try to really *experience* the emotions of that person. If we are able, we might speak back to them what feelings we are experiencing and see if they match with theirs. This skill is the key to effective listening.

Goal—Integration

Remember, we are on a journey to receive the grace—the freedom and power—to exercise each of the functions according to our circumstances and the Gospel. Grace works in nature, so we must cooperate with the workings of the Spirit in our life and must be willing to sacrifice some energy and time to the process. Here we want to emphasize that simply knowing about this material is a far cry from having begun the process of integrating it into our life.

We come to wholeness not in isolation but in society, in groups where we interact with others. This is where our integration and growth toward freedom will be experienced and seen. Our journey is made in community or in families where we live and work. We are called to growth by seeing both our gifts and our limitations. The people that are most difficult to get along with, who seem to annoy us and cause us frustration, are often the targets of our projections and are consequently precisely the people we need to draw us into freedom. These projections—plus working with our dreams—are often the only tools the Lord gives us with which to discover the hidden treasure of our shadow. It is through these community members that God calls us to grow in freedom in the choosing of our behavior.

Dealing with the inferior function is a very detailed and complex process. We have greatly simplified the process to provide a basic understanding and a place to begin. There is much to be studied and to be learned from others. As you move forward, we strongly suggest you use the resources that we have highlighted in the Notes and the Bibliography.

REFLECTION QUESTIONS

1. Based on the reflections of this chapter, which function(s) should you be developing?

2. Which of the suggestions for developing that function seem most practical for you?

3. What other concrete ways will help you in this area?

4. What is a specific plan for the future that incorporates some of these ideas?

NOTES

1. The concept for this drawing is credited to Katherine Myers, daughter-in-law of Isabel Briggs Myers.

2. Marie-Louise von Franz and James Hillman, *Jung's Typology* (Dallas: Spring Publications, 1971).

12

Typology and Prayer

There is a correlation between our personality and our style of prayer. Typology can be a way of growing closer to Jesus by looking at how our prayer and personality interrelate.

We see prayer as being very broad. Any experience that constitutes a communication with God is an aspect of prayer. Whether we are talking about our attendance at Mass, our daily time of prayer, being in touch with God's presence as we look at a sunset or a beautiful flower, or as we serve God in our ministry, all are forms of prayer which make us aware of God in our life.

Typology can help us recognize our uniqueness as an individual. In accordance with our differences we are all called to different forms of prayer. We may look at the lives of the saints or to someone we admire and learn from their style of prayer, but we will probably not pray exactly like someone else. Consequently, it is important that we not judge ourselves by another's standards of prayer. The goal is, as has been said, "To pray as you can, not as you think you ought." Our goal is to identify and become comfortable with our own style of prayer.

Much time and research has been done to match the various prayer forms with certain personality types. We will draw on some of the work that can be found in *Prayer and Temperament* and *From Image to Likeness*. This most helpful approach is dealt with in much more detail in those books.

The approach taken by Fr. Chester Michael and Marie Norrisey, in their preparation of *Prayer and Temperament*[1] is quite
novel. They selected 457 Christians who expressed a desire to
grow in their personal prayer. After identifying their types, the
team spent a year suggesting various forms of prayer to each
and receiving feedback from the participants as to the degree
of helpfulness of each suggestion. From this effort they are
able to offer suggestions of prayer forms to each of the sixteen
types.

In this chapter we will offer suggestions compiled from our
own work as well as the two aforementioned works. We will
cover each of the four functions with suggestions for prayer
experiences and exercises that may prove helpful in prayer and
spiritual growth.

We suggest that the reader pay particular attention to those
functions that fit with both their dominant and inferior functions. As we describe the prayer suggestions for your dominant function—that function you prefer the most—some of the
suggestions should tap into your "comfort zone." These may
be prayer forms that you already use regularly. They may be
forms that fit well with your personality. By paying attention to
the forms of your inferior function—your least developed—
you may find suggestions to aid in your developmental journey.

One of the ways to develop any function is through leisure
and prayer. In using prayer time, you may find that you are
greatly aided on your journey toward developing those functions which you are least likely to call upon. If you are drawn to
a specific type of prayer or want to try something new, ask God
for the grace and help to draw near to him through that form
of prayer.

By being sensitive to the prayer forms to which we are attracted, we might be able to learn more about where we are in
our development. For example, if we had been attracted to a
particular prayer form but now find that it consistently bores
us, it may be a sign that we are being called to develop the
opposite characteristic. If so, the prayer styles of the opposite
may not appeal to us, but the Spirit could call us to try them to
aid in our journey toward freedom. The goal is toward whole-

ness, the integration of all the functions and the freedom to choose any of them when needed. Be careful not to be too rigid with these applications. Don't use only your inferior function in prayer, but integrate it into your prayer gradually and with ease. These suggestions are simply another tool to use in a very complex process.

Some of the prayer forms overlap, that is, different aspects of the same prayer form or exercise may be attractive to the strengths of two types, say, intuiting and thinking. We will offer ideas that are not only prayers, but also exercises that can equally be valuable in our prayer and spiritual growth.

Group Prayer

We will offer some prayer forms and exercises that should be helpful for group prayer as well. These suggestions may be of value to prayer groups associated with the charismatic renewal, RENEW groups, Bible studies, religious communities, and religious educators and parish councils.

We think it is important to the growth of such groups that they vary their prayer forms. If a group finds new people come only a couple of times and do not return, perhaps there may be value in offering prayer experiences that appeal to different personality types. This is the value of having people of different types *lead* the prayer of such groups from time to time. We are not suggesting that a group drastically change its way of praying, rather, that it be willing to add some variety from time to time that may appeal to different personalities.

Introvert/Extravert

Before we move into the four functions, let us emphasize the importance of our preference for the introverted or extraverted attitude.

The introvert will naturally be drawn to more reflective forms of prayer and the inner journey, that is, prayer forms that are more inward and quiet. They usually see God through their own personal experience and through inspirational methods. An introvert may be more at ease with private prayer and worship. Tools such as maintaining a spiritual journal, praying about their dreams, and quietly being in God's presence may be areas of attraction. The introvert's ministry will tend to be more of a "one on one" type of ministry, such as visiting the sick or counseling. They may also be drawn to a ministry that deals with reflection, or much interior thinking, such as writing, and a task that is done with a small number of people.

The extravert, on the other hand, is going to be drawn to more action-oriented prayer. They will often view God through people, events, scripture, and the natural world. They may want to be more involved and act out their relationship with God as leaders, in service, and will tend to be more social- and action-oriented.

The extravert will likely be the person who sees the needs in the world and of other people and who desires to serve those needs. They may be inclined to leadership and organizational roles within their ministries. They enjoy dealing with people and usually like getting involved with them. For this type of person their involvement is action-oriented prayer. In addition, the extravert may be drawn to more communal types of prayer.

As we move through the various forms of prayer, our attitude of extraversion or introversion may greatly affect our personal experience of the functions of sensing/intuiting and thinking/feeling. The introvert will view the functions through the eyes of the inner world and the extravert will see them through their perspective of the outer world of people and events.

Part of the growth process is for each of us, whether introvert or extravert, to see that we are called to the opposite form of prayer if our relationship with God is going to be moving toward freedom. Indeed, we are called to pray and be in communion with God, but we are also called to *action*. We are called to *live out* our faith in the extraverted sense.

We invite the extravert to accept the challenge of Psalm 46, "Be still and acknowledge that I am God" (46:10), and to spend time in quiet reflective prayer. We challenge the introvert also to put their prayer into action, to participate in the outer world of the events and people in their life. We invite them to take the energy gained from their inner world and make a gift of that to others.

It is in this area that we have witnessed the transforming power of the Spirit in Christians. We often see both introverts and extraverts who, after coming into a personal and intimate relationship with Jesus, find the grace to change their prayer styles. An extravert who was never able to take daily quiet time alone with God is drawn to do so. An introvert who would never be able to speak openly in a large group is suddenly able not only to speak, but to openly pray and share in a large charismatic prayer group. Our experience is that these transformations are often very much in step with the person's developmental process as well. We can see the truth in Jung's belief that the first half of life is more focused on the outside world in terms of getting settled in our profession, of raising a family or finding a community and developing relationships with others, while in the second half of life we are usually more concerned with the inner world. We may begin to question what we are doing with our life. We may see our life as slipping away and want to find a deeper meaning to our existence. This longing for a deeper reality, for a new vision, is a longing for God, for the spiritual aspects of life. We find often that those who really take Typology to heart are those who are turning or have turned the corner to that second half of life.

Prayer of the Senser

The sensing individual is the one who lives in the here and now. They receive life through the details and the senses such as sight, touch, taste, hearing, and smell.

The individual senser might exercise the presence of God in the present moment, simply to *be with* God—in the "now" reality. There is an old story of a laborer named Jimmy who lived in the city. Each night on the way home from work Jimmy sat in the back of the parish church for a half hour and seemingly did nothing. After years of watching this faithful procedure, a priest stopped Jimmy on the way out one day and said, "Jimmy, what do you say to God every night when you come here?" Jimmy looked a little surprised and answered, "Well, I come in, look up and say, 'Jesus, it's Jimmy.' Then Jesus looks down and says, 'Jimmy, it's Jesus.' " Jimmy was gifted in practicing the *presence of God.* He was able to sit in Jesus's presence without a lot of words or spoken prayers. This was his prayer.

Sensers might also use their senses with scripture. As you attempt to place yourself in scripture, ask: What do you smell? hear? What color do you see? In your imagination feel the warmth of the sun or the touch of the wind on your face.

For example, in your imagination place yourself in the situation of St. Mark's eighth chapter when Jesus heals the blind man at Bethsaida (Mark 8:22–26). See the people as they bring the blind man to Jesus. Be there with Jesus as he touches the blind man. If you are able, touch the blind man yourself. Watch as Jesus lays his hands on the man and puts spittle on his eyes. See the amazement in the man's face as he is cured. Hear the words of those who speak and the tone of their voices. This is a form of Ignatian prayer which will be covered further under the prayer of the intuitive.

On the more extraverted side, simply *be present* to others and develop your listening skills. Through your listening and attentiveness to others, you may develop the ability to listen to the voice of God in your life.

Look at the Gospels (especially Mark's), and note the *attentiveness* of Jesus. See how Jesus uses his senses. Notice how he touches people, observes their needs, is present to them, and *listens.* Notice in Mark's Gospel, chapter 10, how Jesus speaks to the rich young man. "Jesus looked steadily at him and he was filled with love for him" (Mark 10:21).

Ask for the grace to savor and understand the loveliness of the earth and all its richness. Take time to feel and use your senses. Watch the water, be it a lake, pond, stream, or ocean. At the beach, feel the sand, look at and touch the shells or stones, breathe the air, feel the breeze on your body, see the budding flowers, and listen to the sounds of birds and insects. Take time to look at the intricacy of a flower, the details of its color, shape, form, and fragrance.

In the quiet, simply appreciate the presence of God. Use simple vocal prayer to praise him and thank him. Holding the crucifix, a rosary, or religious picture may be helpful to the senser. Bodily gestures such as standing, kneeling, prostrating oneself, or raising one's hands can be helpful in prayer for the sensing type.

Consciously slow down your pace of life. In the busyness of your day, take a few moments to stop, to be still, to be aware how Jesus is with you in the present moment. Ask the Lord for gratitude, thankfulness, and awareness of the value of the present moment. As you move from one activity to another during the day, pause, take deep breaths, pay attention to sights and sounds at that very moment. This can be a richly rewarding habit.

Become aware of how much leisure you enjoy. Be more attentive to taking sufficient time to relax and "re-create." Develop sensing hobbies which call for attention to detail— painting, carving wood, working in the garden.

In a time of quiet, acknowledge the presence of God, perhaps saying, "Father, you are closer to me than my own breath. May each breath I take deepen my awareness of your presence." Being aware of your heartbeat and other body sensations in a conscious way can also draw you near to God. This and other sensing prayer experiences are found in the beginning exercise of the late Fr. Anthony de Mello's book *Sadhana*.[2]

Groups

If you use scriptures in your group, pick scriptures calling forth the senses, such as the Markan verses mentioned earlier. Perhaps light a candle and have everyone focus upon it. Pass a symbol, like a crucifix or medal or a picture, from person to person so they can feel it, see it, and be present to it. A scripture meditation can encourage participants to use their senses in their imagination.

Prayer of the Intuitive

The intuitive is the one who lives more in the future, cares about possibilities, and is often drawn to symbols and the use of imagination.

For intuitives, focusing on the still point, on the "no" thing, or centering prayer can be helpful. One description of centering prayer is that all of your energy is focused on a word or phrase, such as "Jesus," "love," or "Savior," and you say that word or phrase over and over in the quiet of your mind. When other thoughts surface, you again focus on the word. Your pattern of breathing and reciting the word becomes the center of your prayer.

Ignatian prayer, which we mentioned above under prayer of the sensing, can also be helpful for the intuiting type. Ignatian prayer is truly entering into a Gospel scene as a participant and imagining what it would be like to be there. Imagine yourself in the different scenes and experiences in the life of Jesus.

A suggestion for prayer is to use the scripture of Martha and Mary from the Gospel of Luke (10:38–42). After reading the scripture, place yourself at the home of Martha and Mary. What do you imagine the village to be like? Imagine being there with them. Allow your imagination to come alive. How would you feel in their home? Would you most like to relate to Martha or to Mary? Imagine that you are one of them. What thoughts and images run through your mind as you are preparing for Jesus to come into your home? What are your thoughts of your sister? As Jesus walks in the door, how do you imagine he would look and act and what most attracts you to him? You may place yourself in the scene as Mary, Martha, or someone else looking on. It is important in Ignatian prayer that you take an *active role* and allow interaction between yourself and Jesus. Are there any special words that Jesus says to you? What is your response? Allow yourself to enter fully into the scripture scene. Allow your imagination to be open to all the possibilities the Lord would like to show you about yourself, your life, and your relationship with himself.

Ignatian prayer can be helpful to a number of personality types. For example, by using this method of entering into a scene and using the imagination and looking at the possibilities, the faculties of the intuitive are exercised. By focusing on the Gospel scene and bringing the senses into play, as described under Prayer of the Sensing, the faculties of the sensing type are used. Again, Fr. De Mello's book *Sadhana* can be an aid.

An intuitive may find it helpful to use their imagination in other ways during prayer. What would it be like if I were walking on the beach with Jesus? Or if I were with the disciples in the woods? What would it be like if Jesus came to visit me today?

Another suggestion is to picture yourself at a favorite retreat or vacation spot. Imagine yourself there again and enjoying it, but this time with Jesus. Live it in your mind, sharing it with Jesus—perhaps some special aspect of it. See how he enjoys simply being there with you.

By using the intuitive's affinity for the symbolic, one could focus on the symbols found in the liturgy: incense, colors, gestures, etc. Even the round shape of the host is a symbol upon which you may reflect. Remember, a symbol always stands for something more than the obvious, surface meaning. It is deeper, more significant. Choose an image from scripture with which you can identify and take some time to reflect on the various ways in which it is symbolic of your life.

You may choose an image of a mountain, the sun, a river, or a tree. A tree may symbolize our spiritual journey. As a tree grows, develops, and matures, its roots grow deeper and are more firmly rooted in the soil. So it is with us. As we grow and mature in our relationship with God, our roots become more deeply entrenched in the soil. We, like the tree, go through different cycles and stages. In the fall, the leaves change and fall to the ground. In our lives, we are called to change, to let go and sometimes give up certain things. As the tree is barren in the winter, we too may feel as if the Lord is not present in our life. In the springtime new life appears on the trees, and so it is with us, as we grow and change, that new life appears.

The Book of Revelation and John's Gospel can be appealing to the intuitive within each of us, as both of these books use much symbolic language. John's Gospel speaks of the Bread of Life, the Good Shepherd, the Vine and the Branches, the Living Water, and others. All of these can reflect many different possibilities of deep inner meaning in our life.

An intuitive might picture in their mind the people with

whom they have met during the day and their interaction with them, then imagine them as the Risen Lord himself appearing in disguise. We may recognize the Lord in them and thank God for the gift of his grace and enlightenment.

The intuitive, or those developing this function, may find it valuable to pay attention to their dreams. Our dreams are the voice of the unconscious and are one way that God speaks to us. Write the dreams down in a journal in detail. In prayer reflect upon any insights and discoveries. Dreams are symbolic. Each person in our dreams is usually symbolic of some part of ourselves. For additional reading on this subject we recommend Robert Johnson's book *Inner Work.* [3] In it he reviews in detail aspects of working with our dreams.

Groups

For groups, teachings on the Book of Revelation and its symbolism can help the intuitive members. During a time of sharing, ask members to speak of their hopes and aspirations for the future.

Ask members to share something about a significant symbol in their spiritual life. For example, during the time we were deciding whether I (Bob) would leave my job with AT&T and begin our ministry on a full-time basis, I spent time with my spiritual director, Fr. John Sheehan, to whom this book is dedicated. He led me in a guided meditation with music, and during it I had a sense of a stole being placed on my shoulders. As we discussed the meditation experience, I realized that I had experienced the Lord's blessing to go forward and begin a new pathway for our lives and ministry. Several days later I received in a package from Fr. John a small stole as a symbol of that anointing of our ministry. The stole is now on our family altar and is a significant symbol in my journey. Many of us have such symbols, and these stories can be shared.

Prayer of the Thinker

Let's review the thinker's preferences. They are drawn to the logical and are interested in truth and justice. They are able to organize facts and data.

For an individual with the thinking preference, praying the Divine Office, or liturgy of the hours, can appeal to their sense of order and routine. Thinkers are also drawn to structured liturgy. The sense of order and routine can be reassuring to them. Lack of structure and spontaneity at a liturgy or prayer meeting may be upsetting to the thinker.

When praying, the thinker might look at the society dimension and pray for justice and peace.

A detailed Bible study can be attractive to the thinker. They might also follow the footnotes in a good study Bible such as *The New Jerusalem Bible*. They might study a New Testament book such as chapter 11 of Hebrews. This chapter has many references about the faith of the people in the Old Testament. It would be helpful for the thinker to go to the cross references and see how they are integrated. Thinkers can also be attracted to devout reading of both scripture and other classical texts—a sort of spiritual "chewing" of the word, that is, taking apart a verse or paragraph and finding its deeper truths.

A thinker, and those developing their thinking, might reflect on a spiritual passage where someone is articulating a creed or a charter of life, such as the Beatitudes, Matthew 5:1–12, or St. Paul's "Way of Salvation" in Philippians 3:1–16. Wisdom literature in scripture such as Sirach and the Book of Proverbs might also be appealing to this person.

Scriptural images and symbols which portray God as strong, just, and reliable can relate especially to the thinker, for example, Psalm 68:34–35: "Acknowledge the power of God. Over Israel his splendor, in the clouds his power. Awesome is God in his sanctuary. He, the God of Israel, gives strength and power to his people." Many of the Psalms reflect on this image of God. It might also be helpful to write out short prayers based on your faith in God.

Let me (Bob) clarify a point. Being a thinker, I have very

definite ideas on the aids that are available for thinkers wishing to grow in their prayer. I, and others, contend that the bulk of contemporary literature on prayer encourage prayer styles that are not always suitable for thinkers. As a result, many thinkers have struggled along, believing that prayer that appealed to them or with which they were comfortable was not prayer. In fact, anything that helps us meet God is valuable. Thinkers, and those who provide spiritual direction to them, should be sensitive to the unique needs of this type. The situation is further complicated by the small number of thinking spiritual and retreat directors who provide guidance in prayer.

Groups

For group prayer, there might be a focus on the Beatitudes and Wisdom literature. In this regard, the group could embark on detailed scripture study. Or a group could occasionally or regularly use the Divine Office as part of the prayer time.

Prayer of the Feeler

Let us recall that a feeler is drawn to relationships and intimacy. They make decisions based on value and relationship as opposed to logic.

The feeling type will be drawn to any form of prayer that fosters a sense of intimacy with God. We may go back into our memory and history and review our own story to recall how God has been present in our life and family and through different situations as we were growing up. We may ask for the grace to see God in times of joy and times of pain. We may reflect on times when we deeply felt Jesus's presence, times when we knew of his great love for us and when we experienced his strength while going through some difficulties. Expressing our thankfulness and gratitude to our Lord for the many ways we have felt his presence can bring about a sensitivity and intimacy in our relationship with him.

While the process of inner healing can be helpful to all

types, it may come easier to the feeler. Fathers Matthew and
Dennis Linn's book *Healing Life's Hurts*[4] could be quite helpful.

A feeling type might focus on scriptural lines of intimacy,
such as Jesus speaking to Peter, "Do you love me?" (John
21:15), or to the disciples, saying, "But you, who do you say I
am?" (Luke 9:20). Have Jesus speak these lines directly to you
and then respond to him. When we read Luke's Gospel we can
see that Jesus was a deeply feeling person. In chapter 7, Jesus
sees the widow of Nain whose son had just died. Luke tells us,
"When the Lord saw her he felt sorry for her and said to her,
'Don't cry.' Then he went up and touched the bier . . . and
he said, 'Young man, I tell you: get up' " (Luke 7:13–14). This
is one example of many of such passages from Luke.

A feeler can also use the "Jesus Prayer." One version is to
say the name of Jesus over and over, letting him sink deep into
your body, mind, and spirit. Know and believe that he resides
within you. Pray the Stations of the Cross or the Rosary or any
prayers that foster a sense of intimacy with Jesus.

Spontaneous charismatic prayer is often helpful to a feeler.
When our ministry takes us within the charismatic renewal, as
it often does, we find that 80 to 90 percent of our workshop
participants prefer the feeling function.

The feeler will more naturally be drawn to spiritual direction
or to having a "spiritual friend" with whom they can offer an
intimate sharing of their journey to God. They will also be
attracted to developing other intimate personal relationships.
Feelers might be more comfortable with receiving the sacrament of reconciliation on a face-to-face basis, as doing so may
help them experience the compassion of God.

A feeler may find value in contemplating the mysteries of the
Gospel over time, such as is done in the Spiritual Exercises of
St. Ignatius of Loyola. Be with Jesus as he goes through his
birth, passion, crucifixion, and resurrection. This is accomplished by entering into a scripture such as the infant narra-
tive, and using it for prayer over a period of days or weeks.
Become a part of the scene. Touch Mary and Joseph and ask to
hold the Christ Child in your arms. In scripture or in prayer,
allow yourself to be with Jesus. Desire his presence, hunger for
him, listen to him. Allow him to be with you, love you, speak to

you, console you, and hold you. Allow him to meet those deepest desires of your heart. Respond to him as you would a close intimate friend.

Groups

Feelers can be drawn to groups with lively prayer and praise and plenty of song. If there are Bible studies or teachings, it is helpful to have these reflect on relationships and family. The group might also use meditations that call for intimacy with Jesus.

Summary

All of the exercises in this chapter designed for individuals can also be used by groups. Take any of the suggestions and do them together in a family, prayer group, or communal setting. It is best to have time for each individual to share his or her experience of that type of prayer. In addition, on a regular basis, members of the group could take turns choosing prayer experiences for the group.

We have spoken on prayer and Typology, but we feel that we have barely touched on their relationship, which is so rich in potential for growth. If you are drawn to more, we highly recommend further reading on the subject—perhaps some of the books in our Bibliography.

REFLECTION QUESTIONS

1. Which of the prayer exercises described in this chapter are you most drawn to use? What does this tell you about your personality type?

2. Of the exercises suggested for your inferior function, which do you believe would be most helpful for your growth?

3. Have you felt a need to change your prayer style or pattern recently? Explain. What might this tell you about your development?

4. Reflecting upon the history of your relationship with God in prayer, what changes or movements do you see and how does this speak to you about your growth or need to grow?

NOTES

1. Chester P. Michael and Marie C. Norrisey, *Prayer and Temperament* (Charlottesville, Va.: The Open Door, 1984).

2. Anthony de Mello, S.J., *Sadhana: A Way to God* (Garden City, N.Y.: Image Books, Doubleday & Company, 1984).

3. Robert A. Johnson, *Inner Work* (San Francisco: Harper & Row, 1986).

4. Dennis and Matthew Linn, S.J., *Healing Life's Hurts* (New York: Paulist Press, 1978).

13

Spirituality

We would like to look at some spiritual aspects of what we have found to be a very intriguing subject.

"You have stripped off your old behavior with your old self, and you have put on a new self which will progress towards true knowledge the more it is renewed in the image of its Creator" (Colossians 3:9–10).

As we better understand our behavior and Typology we have the opportunity to put on the "new self." This new self is renewed in the image of God, our Creator. As we become aware of all the aspects of our personality, those aspects we use with ease and those that are still hidden in our unconscious, we can begin to see more clearly this picture of the new self. One way this new life is renewed in the image of its Creator is through prayer.

Many of the saints of the Church saw growth in awareness of self as a gateway to a deeper awareness of God. St. Bernard of Clairvaux said: "The first step in knowing God is knowing ourself."

St. Teresa of Ávila, in her *Interior Castle,* says it this way: "For never, however exalted the soul may be, is anything else more fitting than self knowledge . . . without it everything goes wrong . . . Knowing ourselves is something so important that I wouldn't want any relaxation ever in this regard, however high you may have climbed into the heavens . . . let's strive to make more progress in self knowledge . . ."[1]

This growth and maturity in the spirit is a lifelong process. It is a striving to know God and to grow in awareness of ourself. It is a process in which we truly learn to trust ourself more and more to God and allow him to reveal to us that knowledge of ourself of which St. Teresa speaks.

As this trust grows, we are gradually transformed through his help and grace. We are able to let go of what seems so sure and comfortable—our dominant and auxiliary functions—and our fear of the unknown—our undeveloped functions. This leads to a new awareness, a new freedom toward the fullness of life God intends for each one of us: the ability to choose the function that best fits the situation in our life.

Relax

First of all, relax with this subject of Typology. Don't try to determine the type of your family and everyone else who seems to be a good candidate. Discovering one's type is not something one has done for them. Rather, it is a process one is invited into, to do for oneself. If the subject has been helpful for you, explain to others what you have discovered about yourself. Let the Holy Spirit suffuse them with the desire to learn more.

It has been our experience that each person who learns of Typology learns something different. Some learn a great deal and have wonderful new insights into who they are and the journey upon which the Lord has called them. For some it is the gateway for growing in a new way in their relationship with God. Others find that though the material may have been interesting, they didn't learn a great deal new about themselves. Some understand only bits and pieces of what we have presented here. Thank the Lord for wherever you are. Be honest with what you learned, and be at peace with as much or as little as you've received, but be willing to return to it at another time if the Spirit calls you to a new form of growth.

On this lifetime journey to self-awareness, there are many different tools, and this has been just one of them. If it is helpful to you, praise God. If not, there are other tools and theories which will reveal the different facets of yourself. Learn what you can. Be open to new ideas.

Finally, let us offer the bottom-line value that we have seen in using this material. Many of us have moved through life wishing we were someone else, or somehow different. This began early and had its heyday when we were teenagers. At that time in our life, we couldn't look in a mirror without somehow wishing that we looked or acted differently. After we left those teen years, that wishing didn't stop. For many of us, the subject became more focused on our behavior. "If I acted more like Jack, I could have gotten that raise." "If I were more outgoing, like Sue, I would have more friends."

All of this has to do with our image of ourself. Many of us don't think we're good enough. We think we must change to be better in our own eyes. Somehow we'd be more lovable if we were different.

It is our image of ourself that most affects our relationship with God. It has been said that a poor self-image is the single biggest obstacle to receiving the Good News. We want to "clean up our act" before we will allow God to love us. We want to change all those things that we are convinced make us unlovable, and often our personality tops the list.

The Good News to be found here is that we don't have to be someone else in order for God to love us. He made us and he loves us. He calls us to respond to his love. He simply wants us to know his love for us and allow that love to change us. This is the benefit of beginning to know ourselves better and accepting that we are made in God's image and likeness. God loves us. This is truly Good News. Receive it!

This was the Good News that Jesus came to give us. Surely we are broken. We don't deserve salvation. But we are made by a Father who loves us and forgives us and desires to be in a relationship with us. He invites us to be healed of our desire to be someone other than ourself. It is both our uniqueness and our unique potential that he loves. We need to rejoice in who we are and the potential that he has given us to become even more ourself.

The first step to this journey is accepting where we are. We invite you to learn about yourself. Read more books on the topic. Apply all you learn in your own life. With this under way, you are already moving on. As you work at finding out how God has made you, and allowing the Father to love you as you are, you will discover that you have already journeyed far toward your goal.

NOTES

1. Quoted in John Welch, O.Carm., *Spiritual Pilgrims: Carl Jung and Teresa of Ávila* (New York: Paulist Press, 1982), page 75.

Appendix

Sketches of the Sixteen Types

(in alphabetical order)

Sketch of INFJ

The INFJ is an individual who will most likely rely on their strong inner intuition direction. They may be difficult to get to know intimately since they usually have only a few intimate friends to whom they are willing to disclose their true self. They are sometimes very sensitive and can easily be hurt by others. Characteristically, INFJ's are very aware of others' emotions and at times this can take the form of feeling the anxiety, pain, or joy of these others.

INFJ's like to please, and harmonious relationships are high on their list of ideals. They have difficulty handling constant conflict in their daily life situations, especially of an interpersonal nature. This type is usually motivated by praise and affirmation and is also adept at giving the same to others. They find too much criticism a heavy load to bear, and find it difficult working or living in a critical atmosphere. The INFJ is very determined and is usually driven by their inner vision of the possibilities.

The INFJ's usually take their work quite seriously and enjoy academic endeavors. They are likely to be perfectionists in their work and in their relational lives. As a result, they tend to put a great deal of energy into a project or a relationship.

The strongest function for the INFJ is intuiting, which they tend to use in their preferred inner world. This allows them to be open to wide possibilities as they ponder ideas and concepts. Their use of the feeling function in the extraverted world accounts for people seeing them as quite capable in the area of personal relationships and harmony.

INFJ men comprise only about 2 to 3 percent and INFJ women only about 4 to 5 percent of the U.S. population, but together they make up about 10 percent of the attendance at our Christian workshops.

The INFJ usually chooses occupations which involve interacting with others on a one-to-one or personal basis. There are high percentages of clergy, priests, and monks who are INFJ's. Other professions that are attractive to INFJ's are medicine, teaching, religious education, social work, spiritual direction, and consultation.

The prayers of an INFJ may be quite varied. They usually like to practice many different kinds and often require regular prayer-times each day. Keeping a journal can be very helpful, especially in using it to express strong feelings and emotions.

An INFJ may be attracted to contemplative prayer or prayer that is quiet. They are usually able to recognize and focus on the fact that Jesus dwells within at the center of their being. This can be an area of intense spiritual awareness and can bring them much insight into the stillness of God within. The INFJ may find the use of their imagination a helpful tool in prayer.

INFJ's are likely to be in touch with the depths of God's love for them and, in turn, for others. Sometimes this awareness comes about through much inner healing of memories. Symbolic images and dreamwork may also be areas of interest for the INFJ.

At mid-life, the INFJ may desire to focus on simplicity in prayer and in seeing God by using their senses. They should be still and hear the inner heartbeat, being aware of his presence. This type may find recreation and hobbies that call for the use of their senses helpful at this time of their life. They may also find using their thinking function in prayer to be of assistance.

Sketch of INFP

INFP's are only about 4 to 7 percent of the U.S. population and 5 percent of the attendance at our Christian workshops. An INFP has a very deep capacity for caring and intimacy of relationships. They will go to extremes for persons or ideals in which they strongly believe. They are by nature idealistic persons.

INFP's are flexible, steadfast, loyal persons with a strong sense of independence. They are rigid when their values are challenged, yet are sensitive to others' feelings.

An INFP strives toward harmony and integration of body, mind, and spirit. They will often have a sense of the symbolic in their life.

In their preferred introverted world this type tends to use their feeling function to make decisions using values, relationships, and harmony. Their next strongest function is usually intuiting, which is used in the outer world and is more readily seen by others. This gives them a future orientation where they are capable of seeing many possibilities yet to unfold.

They have a flair for creative writing. Some of their career choices are psychology, religion, counseling, teaching, architecture, and the helping professions.

An INFP likes harmony in their relationships and in their life in general. They are usually deeply affected by any type of conflict that is ongoing and will go to great lengths to avoid it.

An INFP has a strong sense of experiencing God within. They may enjoy meditation and contemplation and prefer to pray alone or silently, with quiet time set aside each day. They seem to be constantly searching for new and better ways to pray and spend that time in communion with the Lord. INFP's prefer a spontaneous and personal response to God and may find journaling a very helpful tool. It may also be valuable for them to keep a journal of their dreams.

At mid-life, the INFP may need to practice and develop logical and rational analysis of situations which will be using their thinking function. They may be drawn to seeing God in the details of creation and the simplicity of their life.

Sketch of INTJ

INTJ men make up only 5 to 7 percent and INTJ women about 2 to 4 percent of the U.S. population. About 4 percent of our Christian workshops are INTJ's.

The INTJ has a way of trusting their great vision of the possibilities in a given situation. They may be analytical and direct in knowing how to handle situations. This type is the most independent and appears to be the most self-confident of all types.

An INTJ may be constantly seeking new ideas, new possibilities, and is attracted to challenges, especially when they require a creative response. Consistency is important to an INTJ in both their work and relational lives.

It may be difficult to read the emotions of an INTJ. At times they may seem cold and aloof, although this is their outer reaction and, inwardly, emotions and responses are constantly going on and are very deep and powerful.

The most important function of an INTJ is intuition, which accounts for their ability to take in new ideas and possibilities. This function is usually used in their preferred inner world. The thinking function, used to make decisions using impersonal logic and facts, is more readily seen by others.

INTJ's are drawn to work long and hard for things they believe important, and in their occupations they usually put much effort and time into their projects.

Some occupations that may be attractive to INTJ's are law, science, engineering, psychology, computers, specialists and technicians in various fields, and teaching.

An INTJ will tend to be logical and analytical in prayer and rather independent. They may prefer to decide individually which types of prayer are best suited to them. Thus, they will need to experiment with prayer. This type is sometimes uncomfortable in group prayer. They may find keeping a spiritual journal helpful. A good amount of quality prayer time is essential for an INTJ and the fruits of such stillness will be an increased awareness of God in their life. The INTJ may be a person of deep spirituality and attracted by the spiritual world.

At mid-life an INTJ may be drawn to see God in the simplicity of creation and in everyday life. Using their senses and focusing on the details in life may be valuable in their growth. Developing close and intimate relationships with others will be beneficial to call upon their feeling function.

Sketch of INTP

The U.S. male population has about 4 to 7 percent INTP's and the U.S. female population only 1 to 3 percent. Only about 1 percent of our Christian workshops are INTP's.

The INTP is likely to have insight in seeing the possibilities, and have precision in their thinking process. They appreciate and seek out statements that are logical. They value intelligence in themselves and others and are often impatient with others who fail to meet this standard.

An INTP has an ability to concentrate and also to gain a quick understanding. They may have a difficulty expressing their emotions in a verbal way and may be viewed by others as difficult to know. As a result they are often misunderstood.

Organizing concepts and ideas is a strength of the INTP. They may appear impersonal and objectively critical, since they use their thinking function to analyze the world.

INTP's have deep convictions for truth and justice and have a strength and sureness about them. Those convictions are more likely to remain internal or to be used in their preferred inner world. This is due to their tendency to live this hidden world more with their thinking function and to live their outer life more with intuition, using ideas and future-oriented concepts, which is the side the world will see.

The INTP often prefers to work alone and quietly without being interrupted. Some of the vocations that an INTP may be drawn to are science, writing, research, computer programming, surveying, and mathematics.

In their spiritual life the INTP will be concerned about doctrine and the truth of the Gospel. This type usually values well-thought-out and direct preaching.

Praying alone rather than in groups may be preferred by an INTP. Reading and study of the mystics or classical texts can be inspirational and helpful. Logic, truth, justice, and conceptional harmony are important to the prayer of the INTP.

At mid-life, they may value the sharing of their experience of God with others. This may be difficult at first but is extremely helpful for them. Cultivating a sensitivity and compassion for those closest to them and expressing that verbally to them is an area of growth and development for this type.

Sketch of ISFJ

ISFJ men make up 5 to 8 percent and ISFJ women 11 to 21 percent of the U.S. population. Together they represent 20 percent of our Christian workshops, and are the largest group.

The ISFJ usually has a deep desire to be of help to others and, as a result, is often involved in service. They aim to please and are usually loyal, responsible, and dependable. Often they are hard workers and take their responsibilities seriously. The ISFJ relates well to other people.

A strength of the ISFJ is paying attention to details, facts, and accuracy. This will often show in the appearance of their homes, both inside and out. Perseverance is a way of life in nearly everything the ISFJ chooses to tackle.

This detail orientation of the ISFJ will be used primarily in their preferred introverted or inner world while they will use their feeling function in the outer world. Thus others will see them making decisions with values, harmony, and relationships as the criteria.

ISFJ's are very much attracted to occupations which lead them to be of service to others. Some fields that may be attractive to them are nursing, teaching, clerical work, bookkeeping, library work, medical practice and other health-related fields. ISFJ's receive much satisfaction and gratification from taking care of the desires and needs of others. They *need* to be needed.

An excellent sense of responsibility is usually a strength of an ISFJ. They like to put their best effort forward when accomplishing a task at hand.

Traditions are highly valued for this type. Family celebrations and get-togethers can be important to them.

The ISFJ is usually able to plan for the future, to save and conserve.

They prefer to pray alone and are usually drawn to silent prayer. Spontaneous prayer may be helpful to this type and also prayer of praise, gratitude, and love of God. They can be drawn to the more traditional kinds of prayer. Certain prayer positions or postures can be helpful to entering into prayer for them and add to their ability to communicate with God. Prayer that makes use of the senses and details may be helpful, such as Ignatian prayer. The ISFJ may prefer a set format in their prayer and may have a favorite place to pray.

At mid-life, the ISFJ may need to appreciate and take advantage of both leisure and quiet time. It may be helpful for them to develop logic and analysis in their way of judging. Also, they will need to be open to change and experimentation with new ways of doing things. They should reflect on new possibilities in their prayer life, especially focusing on the use of imagination and finding new meaning in the symbolic.

Sketch of ISFP

ISFP men make up about 3 percent and ISFP women 4 to 9 percent of the U.S. population. They total 7 percent of the attendance at our Christian workshops.

The ISFP shows their warmth and compassion to others more through what they do than what they say. They are generally quiet and reserved and their deepest feelings are very seldom expressed outwardly unless they are very close to another. They are extremely kind and sensitive to the pain and suffering of other people. They are often willing to go to great lengths to be of help and assistance to others.

This type is very often seen as a hopeful and cheerful person and a lover of freedom. They put a high price on their impulses and see them as the center of their lives. The ISFP is very much in touch with their senses and integrate them in all they do. They may be the least comprehended of all the types since they rarely express themselves directly. Their actions usually speak much louder than their words.

The ISFP is generally more comfortable in their introverted world where their feeling function will process ideas using values, relationships, and harmony. The outside world will see more of their sensing function, where their focus is upon the present and details of their environment.

The ISFP seems to have an exceptional love of nature and all of God's creation, being especially sensitive to animals. They are usually modest individuals and may even tend to underestimate their own true worth and value to themselves and others. Their simplicity is one of their great strengths and seems to be a model for much of what they undertake.

The ISFP could choose a wide variety of occupations. Some examples are storekeeping, surveying, clerical, mechanics, carpentering, nursing, athletics, and technicians in various fields. They may be drawn to the fine arts and choose work in dance, music, or painting.

The ISFP's have a strong feeling regarding prayer. They have a sense of experiencing God within and enjoy different forms of meditation and contemplation. They are apt to have a very intense and personal relationship with God and have deep meaning in their lives. This type may find a spiritual journal helpful to gain a deeper understanding of that inner journey. The ISFP will probably be drawn to prayer in the outdoors, close to nature. They are usually very flexible in their prayer styles and would seem to be quite open to the leadings of the Spirit. Music and art may be helpful to their prayer as well.

At mid-life the ISFP may find it helpful to develop the thinking function. Applying logic and analysis in an area of importance in their life can be both helpful and challenging. They might seek opportunities to speak about—and thus share with others—how God is active in their life.

Sketch of ISTJ

ISTJ men comprise from 14 to 30 percent of the U.S. population, while women are only 8 to 11 percent. Together they represent 9 percent of the attendance at our Christian workshops.

In most circumstances the ISTJ is quiet and serious. They tend to be very dependable and realistic. ISTJ's are frequently orderly, practical, and very logical in their inner and outer life. They prefer things in order and properly organized.

ISTJ's are very thorough people who are interested in details, justice, and practicality. They are loyal and faithful to their families and their business responsibilities, with a tendency to lifelong commitments.

The thinking function rules the ISTJ's outer world. From this comes their ability to make logical, somewhat impersonal decisions. Their more comfortable inner world is more sensing-oriented and can be a storehouse of detailed recollections.

ISTJ's may consider occupations such as protective service work, law enforcement, and auditing. Accounting, electrical work, engineering, dentistry, and administration may also prove attractive.

The ISTJ prefers a neat and orderly home and work environment. They may also find a special interest in holidays and festive occasions.

It can be valuable for an ISTJ to spend a large amount of time in daily prayer. They may be drawn to a structured type of prayer. The use of a spiritual journal may prove helpful to reflect on how they are growing on their journey to God. The ISTJ may prefer to have a favorite place and a structured time for prayer.

Expressing feelings to Jesus in prayer may be difficult for this type but can be helpful in their spiritual growth. The use of Ignatian prayer may also be quite helpful to them.

At mid-life the ISTJ needs to be especially open to the possibilities of the future. They may find it helpful to have less structure and more flexibility in their life. It can be a good time to develop some close personal relationships, with intimacy and sharing on a spiritual level.

Sketch of ISTP

ISTP men make up 5 to 8 percent and ISTP women only 2 to 5 percent of the U.S. population. Together they represent about 2 percent of the attendance at our Christian workshops.

The ISTP is usually quiet and reserved and they are able to adapt very well to different situations. They tend to have a strong capability for facts and details. They desire excitement in their everyday life and are sometimes found to be more easily bored than other types.

This type very often will act impulsively and prefer to communicate nonverbally, that is, with actions.

ISTP's desire to be in charge and are often found as leaders. They have a keen sense of timing, they analyze, and they think with a special inquisitiveness.

The inner life of the ISTP is dominated by their thinking function, causing pondered decisions to be made with logical analysis and facts. Their outer world, which is seen primarily through their sensing function, makes them very aware of their present environment.

An ISTP often shows an interest in sports and outdoor recreation. They may be quite impulsive when it comes to their play and recreation. They like to be free to do their own thing. They are often fearless and are able to take more risks than others.

Some occupations of interest to ISTP's are farming, the military, engineering, service work, mechanics, and technicians in various fields. ISTP's will be drawn to occupations or activities that involve precision in the use of tools and craftsmanship.

In their spiritual life the aim of an ISTP is to have their prayer, reading, and reflection geared to the practical. They are likely to find it helpful having a spiritual director. This may aid them in having a deeper understanding of their spiritual progress. This type seems to be attracted to deep thinking and has an unusual ability to concentrate which can be applied to their prayer and spiritual growth. They will benefit greatly if their reflection is oriented toward a practical end. At mid-life an ISTP will find fruit in developing their feeling function and in expressing warmth and compassion and developing close friendships.

Expressing their feelings openly with another can aid in this process.

Sketch of ENFJ

ENFJ's are people who truly need people. They place a very high value on others and may have a strong tendency to feel responsible for them, especially those close to them. ENFJ men comprise 2 to 4 percent and ENFJ women 3 to 7 percent of the U.S. population. They are about 9 percent of the attendance at our Christian workshops. They are apt to make outstanding leaders in their communities and work or parishes.

The ENFJ prefers to live their inner life more with the intuitive function. Thus they will have a storehouse of ideas and possibilities to ponder. Their outer world, lived with the feeling function, causes them to make decisions with a concern toward harmony, values, and relationships.

They may have a high concern for what others think or want and may have a difficult time saying no or turning away from unreasonable demands placed on them by others. They value harmonious relations with others.

The ENFJ's usually have a very personal approach to life and are often filled with a warmth, radiance, and friendliness. They often have a willingness to become involved with others and are strongly drawn to interpersonal relationships. They may sometimes raise their expectations for these relationships to an ideal level that often cannot be reached.

This type has a tendency to be very good at communicating and may make excellent speakers, with little hesitancy about speaking up in a group situation.

It is possible for the ENFJ to become so caught up in another's difficulties that they may overextend themselves emotionally. They may easily over-identify with another's burdens and take them as their own.

The ENFJ is drawn to occupations dealing with people. They make excellent executives, salespersons, therapists, and are often drawn to the field of counseling. They are good leaders, especially when dealing with people face to face, and can lead group discussions with a certain ease.

The ENFJ usually has the ability to use many different forms of prayer. It can be helpful to take time each day listening to God and trying to discern God's will. They can more readily view interpersonal relationships as powerful events of prayer. They are usually drawn to Bible groups and communal prayer, and often enjoy sharing their faith with others. This person may be inclined to see service-oriented projects as prayer.

The ENFJ at mid-life may need to get more in touch with their interior life. As they have a tendency to be intolerant with their own imperfections and the faults of others, looking at their own strengths and weaknesses realistically may be of value during this time. The ENFJ will find that logic, analysis, and being rational are useful ways of making decisions at this stage of their life. This development, difficult as it may be, can bring about new experiences of freedom in their life.

Sketch of ENFP

The ENFP is usually very enthusiastic and optimistic and sees life as exciting. This type of person strives for spontaneity and authenticity and may be especially capable of improvising in many situations. From 2 to 7 percent of U.S. men and 5 to 11 percent of U.S. women are ENFP's. About 7 percent of the attendance at our Christian workshops are ENFP's.

Intense emotional experience is almost necessary for this type. They are able and willing to help anyone with a problem, as they are very warm, imaginative, and perceptive individuals.

They live their outer life more with the intuiting function and will be seen as highly imaginative and inventive. They live their inner life more with the feeling function. Thus, as they ponder their decisions, they will consider values, harmony, and relationships.

The ENFP is typically a very enthusiastic individual and may find themselves surrounded by others who look to them for wisdom and inspiration. Some of those who depend on the ENFP can at times be overwhelming to them, yet the ENFP may find it difficult to refuse someone or to say no in many situations.

Nothing out of the ordinary is likely to escape their attention. They are not usually passive or casual about their attention, but it is usually directed at a situation or a person.

This type may make very good salespersons. They may be attracted to the fields of politics and the arts. Variety in their lives is helpful, especially in work situations.

An ENFP usually prefers variety in their prayer life. They enjoy praying with others, and good experiences of community and liturgy are helpful to them. They may prefer spontaneous prayer and group prayer. To be still and listen in prayer may be more difficult for this type. An ENFP may very easily find themselves on overload with their active life and find private personal prayer difficult, but essential.

It is important for them to keep a balance in their life and in their prayer. Some structure can be helpful, though too much may cause boredom.

At mid-life this type may find a more regular prayer routine helpful, as well as slowing down their pace of life, becoming still, and listening to God. More emphasis may be placed on the inner journey during this phase, especially in developing the sensing function. Using their senses in prayer and also developing an awareness of the details and simplicity in their everyday life will be most helpful.

Sketch of ENTJ

The ENTJ is a resourceful and enthusiastic person. ENTJ's comprise 7 to 8 percent of U.S. men and 2 to 5 percent of U.S. women. About 4 percent of the attendance at our Christian workshops are ENTJ's.

This type usually has strong leadership potential. They are resourceful people and are adept at solving new and challenging problems. An ENTJ usually has a strong preference for action in their life. They like to get things done. They may prefer operations to move on schedule. An ENTJ is usually very organized and enjoys setting a goal, finding a method to reach it and commandeering the necessary resources. They usually have a wide circle of friends and acquaintances.

This type prefers to live their outer life with their thinking function, thus openly making decisions with logical facts and analysis. Their inner-world use of intuiting causes them to be internally considering the possibilities to life, their career, and the problems at hand.

The ENTJ prefers decisions to be based on impersonal data. They can become very impatient with inefficiency in their life or the lives of others. They are usually able to come quickly to the point and like to stick to the topic.

This person is usually quite confident and tends to be adept at getting their ideas across to others. Language for them is an organizational tool. An ENTJ looks for results and may have little patience with vague plans or poorly thought-out procedures.

Some areas that may be attractive to ENTJ's in a career field are college teaching, marketing, business education, training, economics, political science, and management consultant. They enjoy working with people and being involved in what they do.

The prayer of the ENTJ is usually rather structured. They may find the liturgy of the hours with its structured form beneficial. They will tend to be somewhat impersonal in their prayer life with their dominant function being thinking. An ENTJ may find it difficult to set time aside each day for prayer, but the benefits will be numerous. Sometimes quiet contemplation can be helpful for the ENTJ who tends to live a busy and sometimes hectic pace.

This type may prefer reflecting on scripture or a detailed study of the Bible since they value logic highly. They may also enjoy leading others in prayer. Regularity in prayer, spiritual direction, the sacrament of reconciliation, and a daily examination of their day may be helpful to this type of person.

Around mid-life they may get the urge to expand their horizon in prayer and could be open to trying different prayer forms. The ENTJ will need to develop their feeling function at this time, which may be a difficult process since their thinking is often quite strong. This may be a good time to develop sensitivity and compassion to others, especially those close to you. They may need to think of creative ways to put their feeling function into use.

Sketch of ENTP

ENTP men are found in 3 to 7 percent and ENTP women in only 1 to 4 percent of the U.S. population. Less than 1 percent of the participants in our Christian workshops are ENTP's. They are usually very resourceful people who like to exercise their ingenuity. They are able to handle the complex and are frequently good at analysis. They tend to be very enthusiastic, optimistic, and have a good sense of humor. Others may find themselves caught up in the enthusiasm and energy of an ENTP and seek their company often.

They tend to live their outer life more with the intuitive function, seeing the possibilities in their environment and their inner life more with thinking, internally processing decisions with an impersonal logic and factual analysis.

These types may be quite open to new projects, procedures, and activities and usually have a sensitivity to new possibilities. This may often bring refreshing and new approaches to life. They may have an ability to improvise in their style of doing things.

The ENTP's are usually talkative and have motivating personalities and tend to be lively conversationalists. They may be outspoken and easily able to debate both sides of an issue.

This type of person usually has a lively circle of friends and acquaintances and they consider life an adventure.

The ENTP may be adept in any field or career that is of interest to them. They usually are outstanding teachers, troubleshooters, inventors, or scientists. They often find it difficult to stay with any kind of humdrum detail or routine.

They may like new and fresh approaches to prayer and are resourceful at finding new ways of prayer for themselves and others. Many times a traditional or routine kind of prayer may seem dry and unappealing to this type of person. Contemplative prayer may be helpful, as well as study of the writings of Thomas Aquinas and St. Teresa of Ávila.

An ENTP usually desires a very logical and orderly movement in prayer. When receiving a new thought or insight in scripture or prayer, much of their time may helpfully be spent listening to the insights and allowing themselves to be challenged by them.

A regular prayer time to slow down and listen to the Lord may be especially helpful to the ENTP in mid-life. It is a time to reflect on God and see him in the simplicity of their everyday life and in the details of creation. Developing a sensitivity to others and being aware of their joys and difficulties will be of value to the ENTP. They need to ask God for the grace to develop and grow in deep personal relationships with someone other than their spouse.

Sketch of ESFJ

Harmony, in relationships and in their surroundings, is the key to the ESFJ. ESFJ men comprise only 4 to 5 percent and ESFJ women from 11 to 13 percent of the U.S. population. Nearly 18 percent of the participants in our Christian workshops are ESFJ's. This type seems to be most energized by their interaction with people. They may become very restless, especially when isolated from others. This type is very often a warm-hearted, popular, and talkative person.

An ESFJ lives their outer life more with the feeling function. Thus their decisions will be concerned with harmony and values. Their inner sensing function will make them very aware of their present environment, plus past traditions and experiences.

ESFJ's are outgoing in their emotional reactions and need to be needed, especially by those with whom they are closely associated. If something goes wrong in work or relationships, they may take the blame.

They are usually outstanding nurturers of harmonious relationships in home, school, church, or wherever they are associated. Traditions are highly prized and observed by this type. They enjoy socializing and entertaining.

The career selection by an ESFJ may lean toward service occupations, since this type has such an outgoing personality.

They may also be drawn to sales. They are attracted to "people to people" jobs and may have little interest in abstract thinking or technical subjects.

ESFJ's, being the most sociable of all the types, may be especially drawn to pray in groups. A spiritual journal may be a helpful tool for them and intercessory prayer may be a central part of their prayer. Time should also be set aside to simply listen to God.

This type may be drawn to seeing God in the present reality and especially in the simplicity of their everyday life. It may be helpful to reflect at the end of the day on how God has touched them through the gift of their senses and how God has been present to them through the gift of other people.

At mid-life the ESFJ might begin responding to the inner journey by moving toward less action and more reflection of the interior experiences of God. Time spent on developing their thinking function may be difficult, but valuable to their growth. Their involvement in social justice ministries at this time in their life may bring forth new enthusiasm.

Sketch of ESFP

ESFP's are probably the most generous of all types. They radiate warmth and a positive outlook on life. This type is usually outgoing and friendly and a lot of fun to be with. They enjoy a good time.

They comprise 2 to 4 percent of U.S. men and 6 to 8 percent of the women. However only 4 percent of the participants in our Christian workshops are ESFP's. They tend to live their outer life more with sensing. Thus they aim to miss nothing in their present environment. Their inner life lived with feeling causes them to ponder decisions using values and relationships.

People of this type are usually outstanding conversationalists, having a great joy of life, and are able to create excitement wherever they go. They prefer the company of others much more than spending time alone.

The ESFP can be very generous, sometimes to a fault. They are often gifted when it comes to people and to easing tensions among others in conflict. They may be inclined to live impulsively and yield easily to the demands of others.

This type may be considered to have the lowest tolerance for anxiety and may go to great lengths to avoid facing it in their life.

Remembering facts may come naturally for the ESFP. They are usually drawn to occupations where they can work with people, such as selling, teaching, social work, and the performing arts.

The ESFP, being very people-oriented, will probably find praying and sharing their faith in groups quite helpful to their spiritual growth.

They may enjoy being of service and find themselves being quite generous to others in many ways.

A person of this type can also be drawn to experience God in creation and nature, where they may readily see and feel his touch. St. Francis may be a saint whom they might wish to study.

Different body postures and position can be helpful to this type of person in prayer. Focusing on sacred pictures, using lighted candles and incense may help this type to draw near to God.

At mid-life, an ESFP may need to develop more quiet time to interiorly experience the presence of God on the inner journey. This type may be drawn to a new variety of prayer forms, compared to their younger years. This might include prayer calling for the use of imagination and symbols. The ESFP at mid-life will find developing their intuition of great value.

Sketch of ESTJ

ESTJ's comprise 13 to 14 percent of U.S. men and 8 to 10 percent of the women. Just over 1 percent of the participants in our Christian workshops are ESTJ's. They are somewhat realistic and responsible people who are very much in touch with the external environment. This type likes to see things done correctly and are usually outstanding at organization and in running activities. They may frequently be leaders in many areas and have positions of responsibility.

ESTJ's are usually loyal and faithful people. They tend to be punctual and expect the same from others. They usually have a place for everything and may be neat and orderly in the many varied areas of their life.

They are usually very up-front people who display dependability and consistency in their lives. They may be somewhat conservative by nature.

An ESTJ tends to live their outer life more with their thinking function. They are decisive, with a strong use of logic and critical analysis. This tends to make them less than open to others' ideas. Their inner use of sensing causes them to miss little and to have a firm grasp on the here and now.

Relative to career, they may have a natural head for business or mechanics and a natural inclination toward management.

The ESTJ may prefer a type of prayer such as the Divine Office or the liturgy because of its structure and tradition. They may find the support of others important to their prayer and grow from sharing their faith with others.

The ESTJ may value logic in their prayer. Scripture study can be helpful as they first study and then apply the lesson to their life.

Leading others in prayer can be one of their strengths also. The ESTJ may find studying the lives of saints such as Thomas Aquinas and Ignatius of Loyola helpful in their spiritual growth.

Meditating by walking through the woods, paying attention to the details of creation, and using their senses as a way of prayer may prove helpful.

At mid-life an ESTJ may sense a need to expand their prayer with styles other than they have used in their first half of life. Using prayer that fosters intimacy, such as the Jesus Prayer or the Rosary, may be useful. They might also be drawn to cultivate an intimate friendship with a feeling-type person at this time.

Sketch of ESTP

One word that would best describe an ESTP would be "resourceful." They comprise about 5 to 6 percent of U.S. men and 2 to 4 percent of the women. Less than 1 percent of the participants in our Christian workshops are ESTP's.

The ESTP prefers to live their outer world more with sensing. They take life in through their senses and miss very little. Acting upon their inner world primarily with their thinking causes them to use logic and facts when making decisions.

They are usually men and women of action. They tend to enjoy what comes along and are generally tolerant, adaptable, and conservative in values.

ESTP's are usually clever and fun to be with. There is infrequently a dull moment when an ESTP is nearby.

Living in the present is a preference of this type. They are usually very charming individuals, but they may have a low tolerance for anxiety. They tend to have a unique personality and many times other people cannot comprehend this mystery.

ESTP's tend to like mechanical things, but they are also often excellent as the negotiator or the diplomat. Their careers vary greatly, and they usually prefer a lot of action in their employment opportunities.

Being people of action, an ESTP can relate to the prayer of action. Living out their prayer in their everyday life is something they are drawn to do. They may find it easy to pray while working, driving, and acting in the community. It is also helpful for this type to set aside some time each day for formal prayer, even though it may be more difficult for them to do.

Good experiences of community are essential for the ESTP in their spiritual growth. It is also helpful for this type to share their faith journey with another. Sunday liturgy, Bible studies, and sharing groups can be stimulations to their life of prayer and experience of God.

At mid-life this type may find a quieter kind of prayer helpful, as well as using their imagination and spending more time looking at life's possibilities. They may need to develop an appreciation of the inner journey.

Bibliography

Caussade, Jean-Pierre de, *The Sacrament of the Present Moment*, tr. by Kitty Muggeridge (San Francisco: Harper & Row, 1982).

De Mello, S.J., Anthony, *Sadhana: A Way to God* (Garden City, N.Y.: Image Books, Doubleday & Company, 1984).

Grant, W. Harold, Magdala Thompson, and Thomas E. Clarke, *From Image to Likeness* (New York: Paulist Press, 1983).

Johnson, Robert A., *Inner Work* (San Francisco: Harper & Row, 1986).

Jung, Carl G., *Man and His Symbols* (Garden City, N.Y.: Doubleday & Company, 1964).

Jung, Carl G., *Psychological Types*, Vol. 6, Bollingen Series XX (Princeton, N.J.: Princeton University Press, 1971).

Keirsey, David, and Marilyn Bates, *Please Understand Me* (Del Mar, Calif.: Prometheus Nemesis Books, 1984).

Kelsey, Morton, *Christo-Psychology* (New York: Crossroad, 1982).

Lawrence, Gordon, *People Types and Tiger Stripes* (Gainesville, Fla.: Center for Applications of Psychological Type, 1979).

Linn, Dennis, and Matthew Linn, S.J., *Healing Life's Hurts* (New York: Paulist Press, 1978).

148   BIBLIOGRAPHY

Michael, Chester P., and Marie C. Norrisey, *Prayer and Temperament* (Charlottesville, Va.: The Open Door, 1984).

Myers, Isabel Briggs, with Peter B. Myers, *Gifts Differing* (Palo Alto, Calif.: Consulting Psychologists Press, 1980).

Myers, Isabel Briggs, and Mary H. McCaulley, *Manual: A Guide to the Development and Use of the Myers-Briggs Type Indicator* (Palo Alto, Calif.: Consulting Psychologists Press, 1985).

Sanford, John A., *The Kingdom Within* (San Francisco: Harper & Row, rev. ed., 1987).

Savary, Louis M., Patricia H. Berne, and Strephon Kaplan Williams, *Dreams and Spiritual Growth: A Christian Approach to Dreamwork* (New York: Paulist Press, 1984).

Schemel, George J., and James A. Borbely, *Facing Your Type* (Wernersville, Pa.: Typrofile Press, 1982).

Simons, George F., *Keeping Your Personal Journal* (New York: Paulist Press, 1978).

Von Franz, Marie-Louise, and James Hillman, *Jung's Typology* (Dallas: Spring Publications, 1971).

Welch, O.Carm., John, *Spiritual Pilgrims: Carl Jung and Teresa of Ávila* (New York: Paulist Press, 1982).

Whitmont, Edward C., *The Symbolic Quest* (Princeton, N.J.: Princeton University Press, 1978).